**Every book sold plants a tree.**
**Thanks for your contribution to a greener world.**

This is made possible by:

ONETREEPLANTED

www.onetreeplanted.org

GENTLE VEGAN

# THE GENTLE GUIDE TO PLANT-POWERED FITNESS

- ENGLISH VERSION -

Michael Markens

Imprint

"The Gentle Guide to Plant-Powered Fitness"
English Version


Printing and distribution on behalf of the author:
tredition GmbH, Halenreie 40-44, 22359 Hamburg, Germany

ISBN

| | |
|---|---|
| Paperback: | 978-3-384-08119-3 |
| Hardcover: | 978-3-384-08120-9 |
| e-Book: | 978-3-384-08121-6 |



GENTLE VEGAN

tredition

# Table of Contents

*"Vegan fitness is more than a physical pursuit; it's a journey towards conscious living and environmental stewardship."*

GENTLE VEGAN

# Chapter 01

# Introduction

# The Mission of Gentle Vegan

Welcome to "The Gentle Guide to Plant-Powered Fitness," your comprehensive guide to a powerful and healthy life in harmony with a vegan lifestyle. Our platform, Gentle Vegan, is dedicated to supporting and inspiring people on their journey to a more conscious and animal-friendly lifestyle. We are more than just a brand; we are a movement that highlights and promotes the positive impact of the vegan lifestyle on health, the environment, and animals.

In the following chapters, we will delve deep into the world of vegan fitness, placing special emphasis on a balanced and nutrient-rich diet. Our approach is holistic, based on scientific knowledge and practical experience. We firmly believe that fitness and well-being go hand in hand and that a plant-based diet is the key to both.

At Gentle Vegan, we understand that transitioning to a vegan lifestyle can bring challenges. That's why we offer not just valuable information and resources, but also personal coaching sessions and round-the-clock access to our innovative coaching AI. We are here to accompany, motivate, and support you so that you can achieve your goals and lead a fulfilled, healthy life.

Our community is diverse, comprising people from

all walks of life who have chosen a better world and a more conscious way of living. Whether you are already vegan or just starting out, "The Gentle Guide to Plant-Powered Fitness" is your companion on this exciting journey.

In the following pages, we will show you how to achieve your fitness goals, optimize your diet, and strengthen your body and mind, while living compassionately and mindfully. Together, we will explore how powerful and enriching a vegan lifestyle can be.

## The Connection between Veganism and Fitness

When one thinks of veganism, the aspect of diet often comes to mind first. However, it is about so much more. It is about a life philosophy that prioritizes the welfare of animals, the protection of the environment, and the promotion of one's own health. The connection between veganism and fitness is a vital part of this philosophy, as a healthy body and a clear mind are the foundation for living in harmony with our values.

Fitness in the vegan lifestyle means not just being physically active. It's about combining physical activity with a nutrient-rich, plant-based diet to achieve optimal results. Plant-based nutrition has proven to be extremely effective in providing energy, promoting recovery after training, and enhancing overall health. Athletes like Lewis Hamilton, Venus Williams, and Patrik Baboumian are impressive examples of what is possible on a vegan diet.

Yet veganism and fitness are more than just personal health and athletic performance. They are also a strong statement against animal suffering and environmental destruction. Animal production is one of the biggest environmental pollutants and contributes significantly to climate change. By choosing plant-based foods and maintaining an active lifestyle, we help reduce our ecological footprint and set a sign for a more sustainable future.

At Gentle Vegan, we believe that every step towards veganism and fitness is a step towards a better world. By combining these two elements, we create a strong foundation for a long, healthy, and fulfilling life, while also contributing our part to the protection of the planet and its inhabitants.

In this book, we will show you how to make this connection in your own life. We will explore the benefits of a plant-based diet for your fitness goals, share practical tips and recipes, and inspire you to start or continue your own journey towards a healthier, more conscious life.

# The Benefits of a Plant-Based Diet for Athletes

Switching to a plant-based diet can offer numerous benefits for athletes, positively impacting their performance, recovery, and overall health.

## Improved Heart Health

Plant-based foods are typically low in saturated fats and cholesterol-free. A diet high in these nutrients has been linked to an increased risk of cardiovascular diseases. People living a vegan lifestyle often have lower blood pressure and a reduced risk of heart diseases, which can be particularly beneficial for endurance athletes.

## Faster Recovery

A plant-based diet is rich in antioxidants and natural anti-inflammatory compounds. These substances can help reduce muscle inflammation and pain after training, shortening recovery time. This allows for more frequent and intense training sessions, which can lead to improved performance.

## Weight Management

Many plant-based foods are less calorie-dense compared to animal products, making weight management easier. This can be particularly beneficial for athletes in weight classes or those aiming for a specific body weight.

## Stable Energy Supply

A plant-based diet, rich in complex carbohydrates, can contribute to a stable energy supply. These nutrients are broken down slower, helping to keep blood sugar levels stable, which leads to a consistent energy supply during training.

## Longer Athletic Career

There are indications that a plant-based diet can help extend the lifespan of an athletic career. The anti-inflammatory properties and improved recovery can reduce the risk of injuries, while the overall health benefits can support a longer and more successful career.

## Environmental and Animal Protection

While this point does not directly affect athletic performance, it is an important aspect of the vegan lifestyle. The production of plant-based foods typically has a lower ecological footprint and is associated with less animal suffering compared to the production of animal products.

In the following chapters, these topics will be further explored, and practical advice will be given for implementing a balanced, performance-oriented vegan diet.

## Creating Awareness of Challenges

Transitioning to a vegan diet is a rewarding process, but it can also present challenges, especially for active individuals and athletes. It is important to be aware of these challenges to ensure that the body gets all the nutrients it needs for optimal performance and recovery.

### Protein Intake

As a fundamental building block for muscle building and repair, protein is an essential part of every athlete's diet. A plant-based diet offers a variety of protein sources, and in the coming chapters, we will delve deeper into how you can meet your protein needs on a plant basis.

## Iron and Vitamin B12

These nutrients are crucial for energy and endurance. We will explore strategies on how you can obtain sufficient amounts of these nutrients through plant-based foods and, if necessary, through supplements.

## Calcium and Omega-3 Fatty Acids

These play a significant role in bone health and the body's inflammatory responses. In later chapters, you will learn more about the best plant sources and how to integrate these nutrients into your diet.

## Vitamins and Minerals

A balanced intake of vitamins and minerals is crucial for overall health and well-being. We will discuss how a diverse and colorful diet can help you get all the necessary micronutrients.

## Individuality

Every body is different, and so are the needs of each athlete. This book will help you find your own path to optimally adapt a plant-based diet to your individual needs and goals.

By creating an awareness of these challenges and simultaneously offering practical solutions and strategies, we aim to support you on your journey to a plant-based diet that enhances your athletic ambitions and strengthens your health. The next step in this process will be to dive deeper into the specific aspects of vegan nutrition to ensure you are well-prepared for your athletic activities.

GENTLE VEGAN

## Chapter 02

# Understanding the Various Fitness Disciplines

# Overview of Sports and Disciplines

Fitness is a multifaceted concept that extends far beyond the boundaries of classical weight training in the gym. It encompasses a wide range of activities, all aimed at improving physical condition, promoting health, and enhancing overall well-being.

Each sport and fitness discipline has its own requirements and trains the body in different ways. While some disciplines, like weightlifting and bodybuilding, focus on muscle strength and volume, others, such as yoga or Pilates, concentrate more on flexibility, balance, and core strength. Others still, like running, cycling, or swimming, are aimed at increasing cardiovascular endurance.

What unites all these disciplines is the need for a tailored diet that meets the specific requirements of the training. For instance, a marathon runner will have a higher need for carbohydrates to support long endurance sessions, while a strength athlete may need to increase protein intake to promote muscle building and repair.

In the context of a vegan fitness lifestyle, it is

essential to understand how to optimally use a plant-based diet to enhance energy provision for specific training while avoiding deficiencies. This knowledge allows athletes to maximize their performance while remaining true to their ethical decisions.

In the following sections, we will delve deeper into the world of strength sports, endurance sports, and other disciplines to illuminate how a vegan diet can support and enhance performance. We will look at which nutrients are particularly important and how best to obtain them from plant-based sources.

## Strength Sports and Bodybuilding

Strength sports encompass a range of disciplines focused on building muscle strength and mass, with bodybuilding as a special category characterized by the goal of muscle definition and symmetry. These disciplines demand not only physical effort but also an understanding of the underlying biological processes of muscle building and energy supply.

A vegan diet optimized for strength sports and bodybuilding must be carefully planned to ensure that all necessary nutrients are present in sufficient amounts. Proteins, the building blocks of muscles, are crucial for repair, maintenance, and the construction of muscle structure. Vegans can meet their protein needs through a variety of sources: legumes like lentils, chickpeas, and beans; whole grains like quinoa and amaranth; as well as nuts, seeds, and soy products. Integrating plant-based protein powders such as pea, hemp, or rice protein can also help supplement daily protein intake, especially after intense training sessions when the body needs rapidly absorbable amino acids.

Carbohydrates should not be underestimated in a balanced nutrition plan. They serve as the primary fuel for short, high-intensity activities and are essential for glycogen storage in muscles and liver. While complex carbohydrates from whole grains, starchy vegetables, and other plant materials provide a slow and steady energy source, simple carbohydrates like fruits or smoothies with dates can provide quick energy for training and are beneficial after training to rapidly replenish glycogen stores and support muscle recovery.

Ultimately, it is the synergistic combination of these macronutrients, along with a rich array of micronutrients from a diverse range of plant foods, that enables optimal performance and recovery in strength sports and bodybuilding. A consciously composed vegan diet, supported by evidence-based supplementation, can not only meet nutrient needs but also contribute to increased overall health and a reduced risk of chronic diseases.

A comprehensive understanding of the interactions between diet and training load is crucial for every athlete committed to the vegan lifestyle. Correct application of nutritional principles in the context of strength sports and bodybuilding can support athletes in achieving their goals without compromising their ethical beliefs.

## Endurance Sports

The world of endurance sports is diverse and fascinating. It tests the limits of human performance and requires a combination of mental strength, physical endurance, and tactical intelligence. Popular endurance sports include running, cycling, and swimming, each presenting its own challenges and dietary requirements.

Running, whether over short distances or marathons, demands a lot from the body. Vegan runners need to ensure they consume enough carbohydrates for energy, as these are the primary fuel source during long runs. Complex carbohydrates found in whole grains, legumes, and starchy vegetables should form a significant part of their diet. Simultaneously, it's important not to neglect protein intake to support the repair and growth of muscle tissue.

Cycling challenges the lower body parts especially and can last hours or even days in stage races. The right balance of macronutrients is essential here. Adequate fat intake, particularly from Omega-3 sources like flaxseeds or walnuts, can help lubricate joints and reduce inflammation that can arise from long rides.

Swimming is a full-body workout that places special demands on breathing techniques. Swimmers need a balanced diet with a good mix of proteins for muscle building and sufficient carbohydrates to provide energy for intense water training. Additionally, careful fluid intake is crucial, as the sensation of thirst is often underestimated in water.

For all these sports, it's important not only to focus on macronutrients but also to ensure adequate micronutrient supply, such as iron, vitamin B12, and vitamin D, which can sometimes be lacking in a vegan diet. A carefully planned vegan diet that includes all essential nutrients can support athletes in maximizing their performance while staying true to their ethical and health principles.

In the context of a vegan lifestyle, it is crucial to adapt the diet individually to ensure that athletic ambitions are pursued sustainably and that the body is optimally supplied with all necessary nutrients. Through the targeted selection of plant-based foods and the use of supplementary nutrient sources, vegans can successfully compete in endurance sports while keeping their body healthy and efficient.

In the next section, we will address flexibility and mobility training and explore how a vegan diet can also be supportive in this area.

## Flexibility and Mobility Training

The concepts of flexibility and mobility play a key role in sports, especially when it comes to a vegan lifestyle. Flexibility refers to the ability of muscles to stretch, while mobility is about how joints move. Both are fundamental aspects that must be considered in a balanced fitness regime.

For vegans, it's important to find the right balance between macro- and micronutrients to optimally nourish the muscles and joints. A diet rich in plant-based proteins, as found in legumes, nuts, and seeds, supports the body in strengthening connective tissue and maintaining muscle fiber elasticity. Carbohydrates from whole grains, sweet potatoes, and fruits not only provide energy for movement but also the fibers that promote healthy digestion, which can indirectly influence body mobility.

Additionally, an adequate intake of fatty acids plays a crucial role, as they have anti-inflammatory properties, which promote recovery and support joint health. Fluid balance is also critical; drinking enough water improves the volume of synovial fluid, which acts as a lubricant for the joints.

In flexibility training, as practiced in yoga or Pilates, the body is stretched and strengthened. These practices not only improve the range of movements and help reduce the risk of injury, but they also offer a moment of calm and reflection often neglected in the hectic routine of everyday life.

But it's not just about the physical side; the mental and emotional state plays an equally important role. A plant-based diet, with its high-quality nutrients and phytochemicals, can contribute to mental clarity and improved stress management. This is invaluable in disciplines that demand both mental and physical flexibility.

Moreover, specific movements and stretches should be selected that are tailored to the individual needs and goals of the trainee. It's important to develop a program that not only aims to improve freedom of movement but also integrates this increased mobility into everyday life and athletic activities.

Gentle Vegan accompanies you on this journey, offering tailored advice and support designed to optimize your flexibility and mobility through conscious nutrition and targeted training. With a combination of expert knowledge and practical guidance, you can care for your body in a way that supports and enriches your vegan fitness journey.

## Team Sports and Playful Activities

The world of team sports is varied and dynamic, ranging from Football and Basketball to Hockey and Lacrosse. These activities require not only physical endurance and skill but also strong team dynamics and strategic abilities. Playful activities like dodgeball or tag rugby complement the spectrum and offer varied ways to promote and maintain fitness.

For vegan athletes, team sports offer the chance to strengthen social bonds while sharpening their physical and mental abilities. A well-planned vegan diet can provide the needed energy for long playing phases and contribute to recovery with a quick supply of nutrients after the game. It's essential that the diet includes enough complex carbohydrates for sustained energy, proteins for muscle repair, and fats for inflammation reduction.

Playful activities incorporated into fitness programs provide variety and can boost motivation. They bring fun and lightness to the routine and help alleviate the often perceived strenuous effort of training. This is especially important for those who struggle to establish a regular fitness routine. Additionally, these activities promote coordination and cognitive abilities, as they require quick reactions and decisions.

Gentle Vegan emphasizes the importance of enjoying movement and not focusing too much on the "work" of training. Instead, the focus should be on how this form of physical activity enhances well-being and contributes to the quality of life. Integrating team sports into a fitness regime for vegans shows that physical fitness can be achieved while upholding the principles of compassion and community at the heart of the vegan lifestyle.

With a plant-based diet rich in diverse foods, athletes can ensure their body receives all the necessary nutrients to perform at their best in any team sport or playful activity. The food should be colorful, nutrient-rich, and full of life, just like the game on the field or court.

# Martial Arts

The world of martial arts is extremely diverse, ranging from traditional martial arts like Karate and Kung Fu to more modern practices like Mixed Martial Arts (MMA) and Krav Maga. Each of these disciplines demands specific physical and mental skills and places unique demands on the practitioner's diet and body.

The practice of martial arts requires not only extraordinary physical strength and endurance but also speed, flexibility, and considerable mental discipline. To ensure the necessary energy for training and competitions, attentive nutrition is crucial. In the context of a vegan diet, martial artists must pay particular attention to consuming enough protein for muscle building, complex carbohydrates for sustained energy, and high-quality fats for anti-inflammatory effects.

Vitamins and minerals also play an important role in supporting immune function and accelerating the healing of injuries. Vitamin B12, which is often a challenge for vegans, is essential for energy production and the formation of red blood cells. Calcium and vitamin D are important for strong bones, which are essential for martial artists to avoid fractures. Iron is another critical mineral, especially for female athletes, to prevent anemia and ensure the muscles' oxygen supply.

Hydration is of particular importance in martial arts, as the intense training and frequent weight reductions before competitions increase the risk of dehydration. Adequate fluid intake, ideally enriched with electrolytes, helps maintain blood volume, regulate body temperature, and support muscle functions.

Nutrition planning in martial arts should also consider the timing and composition of meals to ensure optimal performance and maximize recovery. A deep understanding of how the body reacts to different types of food and nutrients is essential. This may mean planning food intake around training, with carbohydrate-rich meals for energy provision before training and protein-rich meals to support recovery afterward.

Finally, it's important to note that martial artists who follow a vegan diet may need to consider dietary supplements to optimize their nutrient intake. Products like vegan protein, B12 vitamin supplements, algae oil for omega-3 fatty acids, and others can be useful to fill potential nutritional gaps and maintain physical performance.

Overall, martial arts as a discipline requires a

comprehensive and well-thought-out nutritional strategy that can be perfectly integrated into the vegan lifestyle, provided it is carefully planned and implemented. A holistic approach, considering both the quality and quantity of food, will help martial artists achieve their goals while promoting their health and well-being.

## Calisthenics

Calisthenics, known as the art of bodyweight exercises, offers a holistic workout experience that combines strength, flexibility, and endurance. This form of training, focusing on exercises like push-ups, pull-ups, and squats, requires no equipment and is thus highly accessible. For vegans practicing calisthenics, balanced nutrition plays a central role. A plant-based diet, rich in proteins from sources like lentils, tofu, and nuts, supports muscle building and recovery. Complex carbohydrates from whole grains and fruits provide the necessary energy for intense workout sessions and aid in recovery.

A key advantage of calisthenics is its versatility in training. It can be performed anywhere and adapts to every fitness level. Beginners can start with basic exercises, while advanced practitioners can push their limits with advanced movements like the Human Flag or Front Lever. The natural progression in calisthenics not only promotes physical development but also boosts self-confidence and mental discipline.

The social component of calisthenics should not be underestimated. Many practitioners find like-minded individuals in local groups and online communities, offering inspiration and support. These communities foster an environment that supports both individual growth and collective exchange.

For vegans practicing calisthenics, it's important to follow a well-tuned diet that provides all the necessary nutrients. This may occasionally require the use of supplements, especially for nutrients like vitamin B12 and omega-3 fatty acids, which are harder to find in a plant-based diet. Carefully planning meals and snacks around training times can help maximize energy and performance and promote recovery.

Overall, calisthenics offers a unique opportunity to integrate fitness and a healthy lifestyle. It encourages individuals to explore their physical limits while developing an awareness of the importance of holistic nutrition that supports both their athletic goals and ethical convictions.

GENTLE VEGAN

Chapter 03

# Recovery and Rest

# The Importance of Recovery in the Training Process

The journey to physical strength and endurance is not only a story of sweat and performance - it is equally one of conscious pausing and restoration. The process of recovery is a cornerstone of success in sports and essential for maintaining the body's health. The ability to recover determines how quickly and effectively a body can recuperate from stress, how resilient the system remains against injuries, and ultimately, how continuously and sustainably progress can be achieved.

In the world of sports, there is a common misconception that muscle growth and performance enhancement occur directly during training. However, the actual growth happens during rest periods, when muscle fibers that have experienced microtrauma during exertion are repaired and strengthened. This process requires time and adequate resources - nutrients and energy that can be provided by a thoughtful, plant-based diet.

In addition to physical recovery, mental relaxation should not be underestimated. Mental exhaustion can significantly impact motivation, athletic performance, and recovery capacity. Stress management through techniques such as meditation, yoga, or simple breathing exercises can significantly improve regeneration, contributing to holistic recovery.

Gentle Vegan understands the art of recovery as an integral part of training. In this chapter, we will explore the mechanisms of regeneration, introduce effective strategies for physical and mental recovery, and show how a targeted vegan diet can support the body's restoration. Furthermore, we will delve deeper into the role of sleep and mental health, providing concrete tips on how to integrate these into everyday life to ensure optimal recovery.

## Strategies for Effective Recovery

Effective recovery requires a combination of practices that support the body after exertion. An antioxidant-rich, plant-based diet is a cornerstone for promoting cell renewal and combating inflammation. Omega-3 fatty acids, for example, from chia seeds and walnuts, are particularly beneficial and can help alleviate muscle soreness after training.

Good sleep is another crucial factor for recovery. Restorative sleep, especially in the deep sleep phases, is essential for the production of growth hormones that play a role in muscle repair. Creating a calm sleeping environment and maintaining a consistent sleep schedule are practical steps to optimize this process.

Incorporating active recovery, such as gentle yoga or light walks, supports circulation and helps to more efficiently remove waste products from the muscles without causing additional stress. Additionally, stretching and flexibility training can help reduce muscle tension and increase mobility. Self-myofascial release techniques and massages are also useful for relieving tension and supporting recovery.

By integrating these methods into daily life, physical recovery can be optimized while remaining true to the principles of a plant-based diet. An individualized approach that considers personal preferences and needs can further improve the success of such recovery strategies.

## The Role of Nutrition in Recovery

After intense training, the body is not only exhausted but also in a state where it can utilize nutrients particularly effectively for repair and building work. This "metabolic window" is an opportunity to use nutrition strategically to support regeneration and promote muscle building.

A plant-based diet can be especially beneficial here, as it is rich in antioxidants and natural anti-inflammatory agents. Dark leafy greens, berries, nuts, and seeds provide not only vitamins and minerals but also phytonutrients that can reduce oxidative stress and accelerate the healing process.

Proteins are essential for the repair of muscle tissue. Post-workout, vegan athletes should focus on a combination of different protein sources to achieve a complete amino acid profile. Quinoa, legumes, tofu, and tempeh, supplemented by plant-based protein shakes, can support muscle building and promote recovery.

Carbohydrates are also important for replenishing glycogen stores. Whole grains, sweet potatoes, and fruits provide long-lasting energy and support muscle recovery. Additionally, adequate fat intake is important, as fats are involved in numerous regeneration processes. Particularly, omega-3 fatty acids from algae oils, flaxseeds, or walnuts, which have anti-inflammatory properties, are beneficial.

Hydration should not be underestimated; water plays a central role in recovery. It helps transport nutrients into cells and flush waste products from the body.

Electrolytes, as found in coconut water or specialized electrolyte drinks, can help restore the balance of fluids and minerals in the body after sweating.

Finally, certain dietary supplements may be useful to complement the diet and support regeneration. These include BCAAs (branched-chain amino acids), glutamine, creatine (also available in vegan versions), and antioxidants like vitamins C and E, which can help protect the muscles from oxidative stress and accelerate healing.

A well-thought-out, plant-based diet, tailored to post-workout needs, can thus make a significant contribution to regeneration. It's not just the training itself, but also the intelligent nutrient intake afterward that determines how quickly and effectively the body recovers and is ready for the next training session.

## Sleep, Meditation and Mental Health

Physical strength is often emphasized in fitness, but mental health plays an equally crucial role in comprehensive well-being. A healthy mind not only fosters motivation and endurance but also improves the quality of recovery phases.

Sleep is a fundamental element of regeneration. During sleep, the body undergoes several repair processes; muscles regenerate, and the stimuli built up during training can fully develop. A plant-based diet can improve sleep by providing the body with sufficient magnesium and potassium, which contributes to natural muscle relaxation and enhances sleep quality.

Meditation is another cornerstone of mental strength. It helps calm the mind, reduce stress, and improve concentration. Many athletes use meditation to increase mental clarity and accelerate recovery. In the context of a vegan lifestyle, meditation can also help deepen the inner connection to the reasons for this lifestyle choice.

Mental health is a broad field, encompassing topics from stress management to emotional resilience. Vegan athletes might face unique challenges, such as dealing with criticism or feelings of isolation. Here, a strong, supportive network, such as that offered by Gentle Vegan, can provide a safe haven. Coaching and community programs not only offer practical assistance but also foster the mental and emotional support essential for long-term success and well-being.

In summary, it is crucial to consider sleep, meditation, and the care of mental health as integral components of a training plan. They form the foundation upon which physical performance and regeneration are made possible.

GENTLE VEGAN

## Chapter 04

# Fundamentals of Vegan Nutrition for Fitness

# Introduction to Vegan Sports Nutrition

If you have decided to adopt a plant-based diet while pursuing your athletic goals, you have already taken a significant step towards a healthy and sustainable lifestyle. A vegan diet offers an abundance of possibilities to provide your body with the necessary nutrients for peak performance and optimal recovery. In this chapter, we will focus on the basics of vegan nutrition in the context of fitness and athletic activity.

It is crucial to develop a solid understanding of the various nutrients your body needs to perform at its best and recover effectively. This includes both macronutrients, which serve as the main source of energy, and micronutrients, which support a variety of vital functions in the body. Additionally, hydration plays a critical role in maintaining performance and minimizing the risk of injuries.

In this chapter, you will learn more about the importance of proteins, carbohydrates, and fats, and how you can obtain these nutrients from plant-based sources. We will also discuss the essential vitamins and minerals that require special attention in a vegan diet.

Furthermore, you will receive practical tips for fluid intake and daily dietary habits that support your fitness goals.

Armed with this knowledge, you will be able to consciously and effectively manage your vegan diet to enhance your athletic performance and promote your well-being. Let's now take a closer look at macronutrients to understand the role they play in your diet and how you can ensure you get enough of each.

# Macronutrients:

# Proteins, Carbohydrates, and Fats

The macronutrients proteins, carbohydrates, and fats are the pillars of a balanced diet and play a central role in energy production, muscle building, and recovery. Especially in the field of fitness and sports activities, the targeted intake of these nutrients is crucial for success and well-being.

## Proteins

Proteins, often referred to as the building blocks of life, are indispensable for building and maintaining muscle mass. They are involved in a variety of biochemical processes and support the function of enzymes, hormones, and the immune system. For athletes, proteins are particularly important after training to promote muscle cell regeneration and enable muscle building.

Plant-based proteins can be found in a variety of foods, and it is a widespread myth that a vegan diet cannot provide enough protein. Legumes like beans and lentils, tofu, tempeh, quinoa, nuts, and seeds are excellent sources of protein. To obtain a complete amino acid profile, it is recommended to combine different protein sources.

## Carbohydrates

Carbohydrates are the body's preferred energy source, especially during intense physical activity. They are converted into glucose in the body, which powers the muscles and brain. Adequate carbohydrate intake is crucial to fill glycogen stores and maintain performance.

Whole grains, fruits, vegetables, and legumes are excellent sources of complex carbohydrates, providing essential fiber, vitamins, and minerals. Simple carbohydrates, as found in sugary snacks and drinks, should be minimized as they can lead to blood sugar fluctuations and contain fewer nutrients.

## Fats

Fats are a concentrated energy source and play a crucial role in the absorption of fat-soluble vitamins such as vitamin A, D, E, and K. They are also essential for hormone production and organ protection.

In a vegan diet, healthy unsaturated fatty acids are found in avocados, nuts, seeds, and plant oils. These fatty acids can have positive effects on heart health and should be a fixed part of the diet. Saturated fats and trans fats, often found in processed foods, should be avoided as they can increase the risk of cardiovascular diseases.

## Conclusion

A balanced intake of proteins, carbohydrates, and fats is crucial to optimize athletic performance and promote quick recovery. Individual needs can vary greatly depending on factors such as the type of sport, intensity and duration of the activity, and personal fitness goals. Careful planning of the diet, and possibly consultation with nutrition experts, can help avoid deficiencies and achieve personal goals. In the next subchapter, we will turn to micronutrients to give you a comprehensive overview of the necessary nutrients for optimal athletic performance.

# Micronutrients:

# Vitamins and Minerals

Micronutrients, including vitamins and minerals, are essential components of our diet that are needed in small amounts but have a tremendous impact on our health and athletic performance. They play a crucial role in regulating metabolic processes, supporting the immune system, and contributing to energy production.

## Vitamins

Vitamins are organic compounds that are indispensable for numerous biological functions. They help the body extract energy from food, strengthen the immune system, and repair cell damage. Some vitamins are particularly important in a vegan diet:

Vitamin B12: This vitamin is crucial for the production of red blood cells and the functioning of the nervous system. A deficiency can lead to anemia, fatigue, and neurological problems. Since vitamin B12 mainly occurs in animal products, it is essential for vegans to rely on fortified foods or supplements.

Vitamin D: This vitamin plays a central role in bone

health, muscle function, and the immune system. The body's own production through sunlight can be insufficient during the winter months or with too little sun exposure, making supplementation necessary.

Antioxidants (Vitamin C, E, Beta-Carotene): These vitamins protect cells from oxidative stress and are particularly important during intense training to minimize cell damage and inflammation.

### Minerals

Minerals are inorganic elements crucial for the structure of bones and teeth, the transmission of nerve signals, muscle function, and fluid balance.

Calcium: A key mineral for bone and tooth structure, blood clotting, and muscle function. Green leafy vegetables, tofu, seaweed, and nuts are good plant-based calcium sources.

Iron: Important for oxygen transport in the blood and reducing fatigue. Plant-based iron from legumes, whole grains, and green leafy vegetables can be better absorbed when consumed with vitamin C-rich foods.

Magnesium: Plays an important role in muscle function, bone strength, and energy production. Nuts, seeds, and whole grains are rich in this mineral.

### Conclusion

Adequate intake of micronutrients is of particular importance for vegans, as some vitamins and minerals may be present in lower amounts in plant-based foods or may not be as readily absorbed. A diverse and balanced diet, possibly supplemented with specific nutritional supplements, is crucial to prevent deficiencies and optimize physical and athletic performance. In the next section, we will discuss the importance of fluid intake and its specific relevance for athletes.

# Optimizing Micronutrient Combination

The combination of micronutrients plays a crucial role in a vegan diet, especially in the context of fitness. By strategically combining foods, the absorption and efficacy of these nutrients can be optimized, which is vital for the athletic performance and overall health of vegans.

### Synergies Between Micronutrients

Iron and Vitamin C: The absorption of plant-based

iron can be significantly enhanced by Vitamin C. Consuming citrus fruits or bell peppers with iron-rich foods like lentils or spinach boosts iron absorption.

Calcium and Vitamin D: Vitamin D enhances the absorption of calcium, essential for bone health and muscle function. A combination of calcium-rich foods like broccoli or tofu with Vitamin D, either through sun exposure or supplements, is recommended.

Magnesium and Vitamin B6: Magnesium works closely with Vitamin B6 to support muscle function and energy metabolism. Nuts, bananas, and whole grains offer an excellent mix of these nutrients.

## Considering Antinutrients

Antinutrients like phytic acid, found in whole grains and legumes, can inhibit the absorption of certain minerals. Soaking, sprouting, or fermenting these foods can reduce their antinutrient content and improve the availability of minerals like iron and zinc.

## Timing and Meal Composition

Nutrient timing can also play a role, especially in relation to fitness and training. Consuming antioxidants, such as Vitamins C and E, after training can help reduce oxidative damage and promote recovery.

Complex carbohydrates combined with protein sources post-workout can optimize energy supply and support the absorption of B vitamins and amino acids.

## Practical Implementation

Daily meals should be balanced and varied to cover a wide range of micronutrients. For example, a breakfast of whole grain cereals with fruits and nuts, a lunch of legumes, leafy greens, and a vitamin-rich salad, and a protein and vegetable-rich dinner could be a good approach.

Smoothies and juices can also be a practical method to combine multiple micronutrients in one meal.

## Conclusion

The strategic combination of micronutrients is a key element in vegan fitness nutrition. By thoughtfully pairing nutrient sources and considering antinutrients, vegans can maximize their nutrient intake to achieve optimal health and performance. A well-planned, diverse diet, supplemented with targeted nutritional supplements, is essential to meet the body's specific needs and enhance athletic performance.

# Hydration:

# Importance and Recommendations

The importance of hydration for athletic performance and overall health cannot be overstated. Water is involved in nearly all biochemical processes in the body and plays a crucial role in maintaining bodily functions.

## Why is hydration so important?

Thermoregulation: During exercise, body temperature increases. Sweating and the subsequent evaporation of sweat from the skin help regulate body temperature. Adequate fluid balance is essential to support this process and prevent heat stress and heatstroke.

Nutrient Transport and Elimination: Water serves as a solvent and transport medium for nutrients and waste products. Proper hydration ensures that nutrients reach where they are needed and waste products are efficiently eliminated.

Joint Lubrication and Shock Absorption: Fluid in the joints helps reduce friction and cushion shocks, which is especially important during high-intensity training or sports that put a lot of strain on the joints.

## How much should you drink?

Fluid needs can vary greatly depending on factors such as age, gender, weight, health status, climate, and the intensity of physical activity. However, general guidelines recommend:

Daily Fluid Intake: Adults should consume about 2-3 liters of fluid per day, with the main source being pure water.

Before Exercise: About 2-3 hours before exercising, drink 500-600 ml of water to start well-hydrated.

During Exercise: Every 15-20 minutes, drink about 200-300 ml of water or an isotonic drink, especially if the training is intense and lasts more than an hour.

After Exercise: It's important to compensate for fluid loss due to sweating. This can be achieved by drinking water and consuming water-rich foods like fruits and vegetables.

## Special Considerations for Vegans

Vegans should pay particular attention to their electrolyte balance, as they may consume less sodium through their usual dietary habits, especially if they avoid processed foods. Electrolytes such as sodium, potassium, magnesium, and calcium are essential for nerve and muscle function and help regulate fluid balance. Adequate intake can be ensured through salty snacks, electrolyte-rich drinks, or by adding a pinch of salt in smoothies or after training.

Vegan foods such as coconut water, homemade smoothies with a pinch of salt and citrus fruits, or fortified plant-based milk can also help replenish electrolytes. For long or particularly sweaty training sessions, a specially formulated vegan electrolyte drink may be useful to efficiently balance electrolyte losses.

## Conclusion

Adequate hydration is essential for athletically active vegans to maintain performance and promote recovery. By considering individual needs and possibly adjusting electrolyte intake, an optimal hydration state can be achieved.

With these nutritional basics in mind, you lay the foundation for successfully implementing your fitness goals in combination with a vegan lifestyle. In the following, you will find some practical tips and recipe suggestions that will make it easier for you to get started and enrich your daily dietary routine.

# Everyday Nutrition Tips

A balanced and nutrient-rich diet is the foundation for good health and optimal athletic performance. However, everyday life can bring its own challenges, and sometimes it's not easy to make the right nutritional choices.

Meal planning and preparation play a central role in maintaining a healthy vegan diet. By taking the time to plan your meals for the week and buy necessary ingredients in advance, you can ensure that you always have access to nutritious and balanced options. Preparing meals in advance and storing portions in the refrigerator or freezer can also help ensure that you have a healthy meal at hand even on hectic days.

Make sure to add variety to your meals to ensure that you get a wide range of nutrients. A balanced plate should include vegetables, a protein source, whole grains, and a portion of healthy fats. Also, pay attention to portion sizes to ensure an appropriate calorie intake, especially if you are pursuing active fitness goals.

Between meals, healthy snacks like nuts, seeds, fruits, and vegetable sticks can help satisfy hunger while providing important nutrients. Particularly, protein-rich snacks are a good choice for fitness enthusiasts to support muscle recovery and growth.

Hydration is another crucial aspect of daily nutrition, especially for those who exercise regularly. Make sure you drink enough water throughout the day and keep a reusable water bottle handy. Be mindful to moderate your consumption of caffeine and alcohol, as these substances can be dehydrating.

When eating out, choose restaurants that offer a good selection of vegan options. If options are limited, it can be helpful to bring snacks or a small meal to ensure you're well-nourished on the go.

By following these tips and making conscious decisions about your diet, you can create a foundation for lasting health and athletic success. In the next chapter, we will deepen our understanding of the different types of fitness training and the specific nutritional needs that come with them.

## Nutrition for Muscle Building

In the context of a vegan diet, muscle building presents unique challenges and opportunities. Protein-rich foods are essential, but they must come from plant sources that offer the full spectrum of essential amino acids. Foods such as lentils, chickpeas, quinoa, and tempeh play a central role as they provide not only protein but also important micronutrients involved in muscle building.

Calorie intake must also be monitored. Adequate calorie supply is required to fill energy stores and provide the "building material" for new muscle mass. While fats are often seen as secondary, they are important for hormone synthesis – particularly testosterone, which plays a key role in muscle building. Good plant-based fat sources include avocados, nuts, seeds, and high-quality oils.

Carbohydrates should not be neglected, as they are the body's main energy source, especially during intense training. Whole grains, oats, sweet potatoes, and other complex carbohydrates provide long-lasting energy and are rich in fiber, promoting healthy digestion.

Meal timing can also play a role. Nutrient intake directly after training – often referred to as the "anabolic window" – can maximize muscle protein synthesis. A smoothie or shake combining proteins and simple carbohydrates can be effective here.

Hydration is also an aspect that should not be underestimated in muscle building. Water is essential for many metabolic processes and helps transport nutrients into cells and remove waste products from the body.

It's also important to keep an eye on micronutrient intake, as these are required for numerous bodily functions. Supplementation with B12, which is not sufficiently present in plant sources, may be necessary. In some cases, supplementation with iron, zinc, calcium, and omega-3 fatty acids – for example, from algae oil – may be considered to optimize the diet and prevent deficiencies.

Finally, the aspect of variety should not be underestimated. A diverse, colorful diet ensures the intake of a variety of nutrients and prevents the diet from becoming monotonous. This not only promotes health but also long-term compliance with a vegan lifestyle.

By following these guidelines, effective muscle building can also be achieved within a vegan diet, strengthening the body while aligning with ethical and ecological principles.

## Weight Loss and Fat Reduction on a Plant-Based Diet

Reducing body fat plays a central role in many fitness goals, whether for aesthetic reasons or the desire for improved athletic performance. The key to successful weight loss lies in a caloric deficit, meaning you expend more energy than you consume through food. However, even within this simple principle, there are nuances that need to be considered on the journey to a leaner, healthier body composition.

A vegan diet can be particularly beneficial for weight loss, as plant-based foods generally contain fewer saturated fats and calories while being rich in fiber, which promotes a feeling of fullness. However, it is important to ensure a balanced intake of all macro- and micronutrients. Along with proteins, which play a strong pillar in the fat reduction process, complex carbohydrates and healthy fats should also be included. These macronutrients play an indispensable role in maintaining energy metabolism, supporting body composition, and ensuring that all bodily functions are supported during a dieting period.

It's also important not to focus exclusively on calorie counting, but to prioritize the quality of the food. Whole vegan foods are rich in phytonutrients and antioxidants, which have anti-inflammatory properties and support the body in dealing with stress caused by training and diet phases.

To maximize fat loss, it is advisable to plan a diet rich

in vegetables, fruits, legumes, whole grains, nuts, and seeds. At the same time, care should be taken to minimize the intake of processed vegan foods, which often contain hidden fats and sugars. Additionally, it is beneficial to consume regular meals throughout the day to boost metabolism and keep hunger at bay.

In addition to diet, it is essential to follow an appropriate exercise program that includes both strength and endurance exercises to support the body in maintaining muscle while burning fat. Such training can increase the basal metabolic rate, which in turn helps burn more calories at rest.

A carefully thought-out approach to weight loss on a plant-based diet, finding the right balance between nutrition and exercise, can not only contribute to weight reduction but also promote well-being and overall health.

## Specialized Nutrition Plans and Strategies

The individuality of each person often requires specialized nutritional approaches to achieve personal fitness goals. Whether for the ambitious athlete, the recreational bodybuilder, or the endurance sports enthusiast, tailored nutrition plans can make a difference. It's not just about macro- and micronutrients, but also about the timing of food intake and the specific needs arising from each fitness activity.

Within a vegan diet, specialized nutrition plans can consider the following aspects:

### Targeted Macronutrient Distribution

Depending on activities and goals, the ratio of proteins, carbohydrates, and fats can vary. For example, strength athletes generally need more protein for muscle repair and synthesis, while endurance athletes may prefer a higher proportion of carbohydrates for sustained energy.

### Energy and Nutrient Timing

Aligning food intake with training can optimize performance and accelerate recovery. A pre-workout snack rich in carbohydrates can provide the necessary energy for a workout session, while a post-workout meal combining protein and carbohydrates supports recovery processes.

### Supplementation

Although a well-planned vegan diet delivers most

necessary nutrients, in some cases supplements like vitamin B12, iron, omega-3 fatty acids from algae oil, and vitamin D can be helpful to prevent potential deficiencies and enhance overall performance.

### Phase-Specific Diet Strategies

Depending on the goal, different phases, such as bulking and cutting phases in bodybuilding, can be associated with different caloric needs. In a bulking phase, a caloric surplus is aimed for building muscle mass, while a caloric deficit is necessary in a cutting phase to reduce body fat.

### Dealing with Nutritional Challenges

Each person reacts differently to various foods and diets. Some may be sensitive to certain foods or have difficulty eating enough to meet their caloric needs. Specialized nutrition plans can help identify and address such challenges.

### Adaptability and Flexibility

While a structured nutrition plan can be beneficial, it's also important that it's flexible enough to adapt to changing circumstances, such as travel, special occasions, or changes in the training plan.

A specialized nutrition plan is not a rigid dogma but a dynamic tool that should be developed further with ongoing experience and feedback. The goal is a sustainable diet that nourishes the body, supports athletic performance, and aligns with the ethical values of veganism. Gentle Vegan understands this dynamic and therefore offers personalized coaching programs tailored to the specific needs of each individual. These programs consider not only individual nutrient requirements but also personal preferences and life circumstances.

Gentle Vegan's coaching offerings encompass a range of support options: from personal consultation sessions to detailed nutrition plans that are adjusted at regular intervals. Additionally, Gentle Vegan provides access to an innovative coaching AI, available around the clock to answer questions and offer guidance. This combination of personal care and technological support enables Gentle Vegan to ensure holistic support on the journey to a healthier and ethically oriented fitness lifestyle.

GENTLE VEGAN

# Chapter 05

# Tailoring Your Diet to Your Fitness Goals

# Personalized Nutrition Plans

At the heart of targeted training and nutrition is the realization that every body is unique – necessitating an individually tailored approach. Personalized nutrition plans are not just a fad but a crucial component on the path to optimal fitness and health. In this chapter, we explore how you can adapt your vegan dietary habits to optimally support your individual fitness goals, metabolic peculiarities, and life circumstances.

## Fundamentals of Personalized Nutrition Plans

The art of personalizing a nutrition plan begins with understanding one's goals. Whether it's about building muscle, increasing endurance, or fat reduction, the food we consume serves as fuel for these specific goals. A tailor-made plan considers a variety of factors, including age, gender, current health status, activity level, and even food preferences and dislikes.

## Considering Individual Metabolic Rate

A cornerstone of personalization is understanding one's metabolism, which influences how quickly and efficiently your body converts food into energy. Some people burn calories faster than others, meaning they need more food to maintain their energy levels, while others may need to be more cautious with calorie intake.

## Adapting to Lifestyle

Nutrition should not only suit the body but also the lifestyle. An office worker with a sedentary job will have different nutritional needs than a professional athlete. Likewise, someone who regularly trains in the early morning will need a different nutrition plan than someone active late at night.

## The Role of Allergies and Intolerances

When developing a personalized nutrition plan, food allergies and intolerances must not be neglected. Thanks to medical advances and the accessibility of specialized tests, intolerances and allergies can now be identified more precisely than ever before. These tests are a valuable aid in recognizing potentially problematic foods that might otherwise trigger inflammation, digestive issues, or other adverse reactions in the body. A tailored nutrition plan takes into account the results of such tests to ensure that the diet is not only nutrient-rich and goal-oriented but also tolerable and beneficial for well-being.

## Feedback Loops and Adjustments

Creating a personalized nutrition plan is just the beginning. Its true value lies in continuous adaptation and fine-tuning based on your body's feedback.

Feedback loops are essential to identify what works well and what may need to be changed.

A practical method for making such adjustments is the regular review and assessment of your dietary habits, training performance, and overall well-being. Through these feedback loops, you can discern how your body responds to certain foods or dietary approaches and make adjustments accordingly.

Gentle Vegan supports this approach through its resource-rich platform, not only facilitating the transition to a vegan diet but also promoting the sustainability and individual adaptability of the diet. Through a mix of personal coaching, intuitive resources, and a supportive community, a space is created where members learn to align their nutrition plans with the rhythm of their lives.

Ultimately, it's your personal experiences – whether it's increased energy levels, improved recovery times, or a general sense of well-being – that provide the best indicator of your nutrition plan's effectiveness. By remaining open to adjustments and utilizing the tools offered by Gentle Vegan, you can develop a diet that meets not only your physical but also your mental needs.

# Adjustments for Competition Preparation

Preparing for a competition requires a careful and strategic approach to nutrition that goes beyond everyday fitness nutrition. For athletes who follow a vegan diet, an additional dimension is added: they must ensure that their diet not only provides the necessary energy for intense training but also all essential nutrients for optimal performance and quick recovery.

In the context of competition preparation, nutrition must be specifically tailored to the particular demands of the sport, the phase of preparation, and the individual athlete's metabolism. It's important to optimize the timing of food intake, consider the quality of the foods, and balance the intake of macro- and micronutrients. Calorie counting, macronutrient distribution, and micronutrient timing play a central role in bringing the body into the best possible condition for competition day.

Carbohydrate loading, also known as 'carb-loading,' can be significant in the days leading up to an endurance competition to maximize glycogen stores. Protein intake must be carefully planned to support muscle maintenance and repair, while fat, as a dense energy source, should not be neglected, though in a measure that does not impair digestion and lightness in competition.

Hydration should also be re-evaluated, as it is crucial for maintaining performance and can vary depending on competition conditions. Electrolyte balance is key here, especially in long or particularly strenuous events where sweat losses are significant.

Last but not least, the psychological component of nutrition should not be underestimated. Mental attitude and confidence in one's nutritional strategy can have a significant impact on competition performance. Therefore, the diet should not only be physiologically appropriate but also psychologically supportive, providing the athlete with security and promoting well-being.

## Nutritional Strategies for Different Training Intensities

The energy and nutrient needs of an athlete can vary significantly depending on the intensity and duration of training. The challenge is to develop a nutrition strategy that supports the body during high-intensity sessions and optimizes recovery phases. For the vegan athlete, this means choosing and combining plant-based foods to cover a complete spectrum of nutrients.

At low training intensity - such as during long, steady endurance runs or regenerative training sessions - the body will use more fat as an energy source. In these phases, the focus should be on a balanced intake of healthy fats, for example from avocados, nuts, and seeds. Complex carbohydrates remain an important part of the diet, but they don't need to be replenished as aggressively as during more intense training sessions.

Medium training intensity requires a balanced mix of macronutrients. Here, the body will burn both carbohydrates and fats. A varied diet including whole grains, legumes, tofu, tempeh, fruits, and vegetables can provide the necessary energy and promote recovery.

At high training intensity, as occurs during interval training or competitions, the need for quickly available carbohydrates increases. Foods that provide fast energy, such as fruits, white rice, or potatoes, are needed. However, proteins are also important for muscle repair and growth. Here, protein-rich snacks like lentil patties, pea or rice protein-based shakes, and high-quality vegan protein bars may come into play.

In all training phases, adequate fluid and micronutrient intake is crucial. With longer and more intense exertion, the need for certain vitamins and minerals, such as vitamin C and iron, may increase to support oxygen transport and immune function. Again, it's important to focus on a diverse and colorful diet that contains many antioxidants and phytonutrients.

Another key element of the nutritional strategy for different training intensities is the timing of food intake. The period before and after training plays a significant role in how effectively the body can convert food into energy and regenerate muscle tissue. A light, carbohydrate-rich snack before training can provide the necessary energy, while a meal with a good ratio of protein to carbohydrates after training promotes recovery.

In conclusion, there is no one-size-fits-all solution. Each athlete must find out through experimentation and fine-tuning which foods and timing strategies are best suited for their individual needs and the specific requirements of the respective training intensity.

# Monitoring and Adjusting Nutrition Over Time

An effective fitness routine is more than just training and diet in the present; it's an evolving narrative that spans weeks, months, and years. Continuous monitoring and adjustment of your diet are key to long-term success and health. Think of it as reading and adjusting your sails on a long sailing journey – you must constantly respond to changes in the wind and water.

Initially, keeping a nutrition diary may seem like a nautical logbook, where you record not only what you eat but also how you feel. This diary becomes a reflection of your eating habits and reveals where adjustments are needed. Over time, you will learn to interpret the signals of your body – the tide of your energy, the ebb of your hunger, and the subtle currents of your well-being.

Recording your fitness performance is another tool in your navigation kit. The relationship between your diet and your progress in the gym or on the running track is often a clear sign of whether you are on the right course. A plateau phase or a decrease in performance can signal the need for changes in your nutritional strategy.

Moreover, measuring biometric data is like checking your navigation instruments. Regular measurements of your body composition, blood values, and other health-related data points can give you detailed insights into your health status and help fine-tune the finer aspects of your diet.

Ultimately, it's about adapting your diet over time based on collected data and experiences. This is a cycle of observation, adjustment, and re-observation – a feedback loop that leads you to an ever more precise alignment of your diet with your lifestyle and goals. Just as the experienced sailor knows that no single course is suitable for every journey, you recognize that your diet must be flexible, adapted to the changing conditions of your life and fitness goals.

GENTLE VEGAN

Chapter 06

# Practical Application: Meals and Nutrition Plans

# Introduction to Practical Vegan Nutrition

A powerful and nutritious meal is the cornerstone for any fitness enthusiast who embraces a vegan lifestyle. The key lies in the right combination of macronutrients, which not only provide the necessary energy to tackle workouts but also allow for quick and efficient recovery. Here, we will focus on recipes that meet all these requirements and are also tasty and varied.

It starts with a foundation of understanding how to balance proteins, carbohydrates, and fats in harmony to optimize energy levels and promote muscle building. Furthermore, we will discuss the importance of vitamins, minerals, and phytonutrients, which can influence not only physical but also mental performance.

Next, we present a range of ingredients essential in a vegan fitness kitchen. We demonstrate how to cleverly combine these ingredients to create flavorful and nutrient-rich meals. This includes examples of:

Protein-rich breakfast options that include tofu, tempeh, or legumes.

Energy-packed lunch dishes using complex carbohydrates from quinoa, whole grains, or sweet potatoes.

Light yet satisfying evening meals high in omega-3 fatty acids from nuts and seeds.

Additionally, we discuss the art of meal preparation to ensure high-quality nutrition even during hectic times. We round off the chapter with practical tips on how to save time without sacrificing variety and enjoyment.

The aim of this section is to equip you with the tools to develop your own recipes tailored to your individual needs as a vegan athlete.

## Nutrition Plans for Different Fitness Goals

Tailoring your nutrition plan to your personal fitness goals is a dynamic process. Every body responds differently, and what works for one person may be less effective for another. After laying the theoretical foundations for a wholesome, plant-based diet and discussing the importance of macro- and micronutrients, the focus now shifts to the practical implementation and fine-tuning of these plans.

For muscle building, we go beyond the basics of protein-rich foods and consider the timing of nutrient intake. How can you arrange your meals around your training to maximize muscle protein synthesis? We look at the role of amino acid profiles in plant-based proteins and how combinations of different protein sources can support muscle building.

In weight reduction, the focus is on creating a diet plan that is not only calorie-controlled but also varied and satisfying. It's important that weight loss does not come at the expense of your vitality. We provide you with strategies on how to increase the volume and nutrient density of your meals without sacrificing taste and satisfaction.

For general health and well-being, we focus on how you can increase the diversity of your diet to consume a variety of antioxidants and phytonutrients. We show you how small adjustments, like incorporating certain spices or regularly changing the types of vegetables, can not only achieve health benefits but also discover new flavors.

Fluid intake is considered in all plans, with special emphasis on the quality of beverages. Water remains the drink of choice, but we also present recipes for nutrient-rich smoothies and aromatic herbal teas that support nutrient intake and enhance well-being.

Cooperation with Gentle Vegan offers the opportunity to develop a nutrition plan tailored to your individual needs based on comprehensive consultation and assessment. This ensures you receive a plan as unique as yourself and helps you reach your goals in a healthy, satisfying, and sustainable manner.

# Adjustments for Special Needs and Challenges

The individuality of each person shapes their path to healthy vegan nutrition, especially when it comes to fitness. In this chapter, we focus on specific requirements and challenges that can influence nutritional planning. It's about how we can flexibly adjust nutritional plans to accommodate allergies, intolerances, individual metabolic conditions, and the diversity of daily life.

## Allergies and Intolerances

Allergies and intolerances are an increasingly common concern that must be considered in nutritional planning. Vegan diets naturally offer some advantages, as many allergens such as dairy products and eggs are not included. However, potential allergens like nuts, soy, or gluten can still exist within the variety of vegan foods.

Individualized Substitution: A key to adjustment for allergies is finding alternative protein sources. For instance, tofu for soy allergens can be replaced with lupine or pea protein. In the case of a nut allergy, seeds like pumpkin or sunflower can serve as alternatives.

Using a food diary can be helpful to identify and adequately respond to allergies and intolerances. Documenting the body's reaction to certain foods over a period can be an effective means, in conjunction with elimination diets, for identifying intolerances.

Diversity in Focus: The goal is to obtain a wide range of nutrients from different sources. We show how to experiment with versatile ingredients like quinoa, amaranth, and pseudo-cereals to achieve a complete nutritional profile despite restrictions.

## Metabolic Conditions

Metabolic conditions like diabetes or thyroid disorders require particularly fine-tuning of the diet. The art lies in regulating blood sugar levels and balancing energy metabolism.

Carbohydrate Management: We introduce strategies for integrating complex carbohydrates from vegetables, whole grains, and legumes in balance with personal energy needs and medical requirements. It is essential that such dietary adjustments be made in close consultation with health experts to ensure optimal support and safety.

Micronutrient Focus: A balanced micronutrient household supports metabolism and can alleviate the symptoms of some metabolic diseases. We explain how a targeted selection of foods can prevent deficiencies and enhance well-being.

## Challenges in Daily Life

Lack of time, professional stress, or traveling can make it difficult to implement a structured nutritional plan. Therefore, we offer solutions and alternatives that can be integrated into everyday life.

Quick and Nutrient-Rich Meals: A repertoire of quick, simple recipes that can be prepared and taken along guarantees nutritious provision even during hectic times.

Flexible Snacking: We present a selection of snacks that not only provide energy but also meet certain nutrient requirements, which can be easily consumed between meetings or while traveling.

The adaptability of a vegan nutrition plan is one of its strengths. Gentle Vegan commits to supporting you on this journey and providing individual solutions that promote your health and well-being. With personalized consultation sessions and individual support, we ensure that each plan reflects not only your nutritional needs but also your lifestyle.

## Nutrient-Rich Meals for Optimal Fitness

A balanced vegan diet provides strength and energy for fitness enthusiasts and supports an active lifestyle. Starting with a strengthening breakfast, through nutrient-rich lunches and snacks, to a wholesome dinner – in this subchapter, we will illuminate how versatile plant-based meals can enhance physical performance and contribute to recovery.

### Breakfast – The Morning Energy Boost

A powerful start to the day is essential for fitness enthusiasts. A balanced vegan breakfast supplies the body with the necessary macro and micronutrients needed for upcoming challenges. Here are four diverse breakfast ideas that provide energy and are easy to prepare:

Protein-rich Tofu Scramble: Sautéed tofu, seasoned with turmeric, black salt (Kala Namak) for an egg-like taste, enriched with spinach, mushrooms, and tomatoes, offers a protein-rich breakfast. Adding avocado provides healthy fats and makes this dish a satisfying start to the day.

Quinoa Porridge with Nuts and Berries: Quinoa, an excellent plant-based protein source, is an alternative to traditional oatmeal. Cooked with almond or soy milk and topped with walnuts, flaxseeds, and a selection of berries, this breakfast offers a mix of complex carbohydrates, proteins, and essential fatty acids.

Whole Grain Bread with Avocado and Plant-based Spread: A slice of whole-grain bread with a generous layer of avocado and a plant-based spread like hummus or vegan cream cheese alternative is rich in fiber and healthy fats. This simple yet nutritious breakfast is perfect for days when time is short.

Superfood Smoothie Bowl: Start with a smoothie bowl made from mixed berries, bananas, spinach, and plant-based protein, such as pea or hemp protein. Topped with chia seeds, goji berries, and cacao nibs, this bowl is an antioxidant powerhouse that supports recovery after a morning workout.

Each of these breakfast dishes is designed to provide the body with a balanced mix of macro and micronutrients. They are crafted to fit easily into any routine, helping to keep energy levels high and recovery times low.

## Lunch – Fuel for the Day

Lunch is an excellent opportunity to recharge the body after a potentially intense morning. Here are four diverse and nutritionally balanced vegan lunch options:

Lentil Salad with Fresh Vegetables: Lentils are an excellent protein source and particularly filling. A colorful salad made of green or brown lentils, diced with bell peppers, cucumbers, tomatoes, and a dressing of olive oil and lemon juice, offers a meal full of proteins, fibers, and vitamins.

Chickpea Curry with Whole Grain Rice: Chickpeas provide not only proteins but also essential minerals like iron and phosphorus. In a curry with a tomato-coconut milk base, enriched with spices like cumin and coriander, served with whole grain rice, this dish is a treat for the taste buds and a source of energy for the body.

Vegetable Wraps with Tofu and Avocado Cream: Thin whole-grain wraps filled with roasted tofu, spinach, grated carrot, and avocado cream are a quick, nutrient-rich lunch that can be easily transported – ideal for on-the-go or the office.

Vegan Sushi with Quinoa and Vegetable Filling: Instead of white rice, quinoa can provide a protein-rich base for sushi. Combined with a filling of avocado, cucumber, sweet potato, and bell pepper, rolled in Nori sheets, it makes a delicious and original meal.

These lunch meals are designed to provide the body with sustainable energy while being easily digestible so that you don't feel heavy and sluggish but ready for the afternoon's activities.

## Snacks – For the Small Hunger in Between

Snacks are essential to boost metabolism and maintain constant energy levels. Here are four nutritious snack options:

Roasted Chickpeas: Spicy and crunchy, they are a perfect snack for in-between. They offer a good portion of protein and are an excellent alternative to chips.

Energy Balls with Dates and Nuts: Small power packs made from pureed dates, ground almonds or cashews, perhaps some cocoa or vanilla for extra flavor, provide quick energy and help against the afternoon slump.

Fruit with Nut Butter: Apple slices or bananas

with a dollop of almond or peanut butter offer a tasty combination of fast and slow carbohydrates and healthy fats.

Vegetable Sticks with Hummus: Carrots, cucumbers, or bell peppers cut into strips and dipped in hummus are not only tasty but also rich in fibers and proteins.

These snacks are composed to not only satisfy hunger but also contribute to muscle recovery and provide the body with important nutrients.

## Dinner – Nourishing Rest Phase

Dinner concludes the day and prepares the body for the recovery phase during sleep. It's important that this meal is nourishing and calming but doesn't sit too heavily in the stomach. Here are four balanced vegan dinners:

Baked Sweet Potato and Chickpea Casserole: The sweet potato, rich in carbohydrates and fibers, combined with the protein of chickpeas and a light tomato sauce, creates a dish that fills without being burdensome.

Vegan Chili with Quinoa: A hearty chili made from black beans, corn, and bell peppers, served over quinoa, is packed with proteins and also a comfort dish that is particularly warming and soothing in the cooler months.

Zoodles (Zucchini Noodles) with Avocado Pesto: A lighter alternative to traditional pasta, zoodles combined with a rich pesto made from avocado, basil, and pine nuts offer a meal rich in nutrients and healthy fats.

Asian Vegetable Stir-Fry with Tofu: A stir-fry of broccoli, bell peppers, carrots, and tofu in a soy sauce-sesame marinade is quickly prepared, versatile, and provides a good balance of proteins, fats, and carbohydrates.

These dinner meals are consciously chosen to not overburden the body, yet satisfy and provide the necessary macro and micronutrients for nocturnal regeneration.

# Summary and Tips for Implementation

Implementing a vegan diet that is compassionate towards animals and the environment, while also supporting your fitness goals, can initially be a challenge. However, with the right approach, it becomes a fulfilling habit that benefits your body and mind. In this section, we summarize the key points and offer practical strategies to help you seamlessly integrate your new nutritional plans into your daily life and maintain them in the long term.

Set Realistic Goals: Start with clear, achievable goals that fit your lifestyle. If you are new to veganism and fitness, don't try to change everything at once. Instead, focus on making gradual changes and monitoring your progress.

Planning is Crucial: Plan your meals and snacks in advance. This not only helps resist temptations but also ensures that you receive all the nutrients you need. Use the recipe suggestions and nutrition plans from previous sections as a basis for your weekly shopping and cooking routines.

Preparation is Everything: Meal prep can be a game-changer. By preparing meals in advance, you save time and ensure that you eat healthily even on hectic days. Experiment with different recipes to find out what tastes best to you and what is most practical.

Integration into Daily Life: Find ways to integrate your new diet into your everyday life. This may mean exploring vegan options in restaurants or learning how to veganize favorite dishes. The flexibility that veganism can offer will surprise you.

Seek Support: It's easier to stick to your goals with support from friends, family, or a community. Join vegan groups, share your experiences, and learn from others. Gentle Vegan also offers a coaching program that you can use if you need individual support.

Think Long Term: Always remind yourself of the reasons for your decision. Whether it's for your health, animal welfare, or the environment – remember your motivation, especially in moments of weakness.

Stay Flexible: Don't be too strict with yourself. A flexible approach can help you not feel overwhelmed and maintain your new diet permanently. If you have a day when things don't go as planned, accept it and continue the next day.

Education is Essential: Stay curious and continue learning. Read books, watch documentaries, and follow experts in vegan nutrition and fitness. Knowledge is a powerful resource that will help you make informed decisions and continuously improve your diet.

With these tips and the right attitude, adopting a vegan lifestyle that supports your fitness will become an enjoyable and rewarding journey. Remember that every meal is a chance to choose for your health, the animals, and the planet. Stay patient and positive, and enjoy every step of this path.

GENTLE VEGAN

## Chapter 07

# Practical Application: Training and Workout Plans

# The Interplay of Nutrition and Exercise

When it comes to fitness and health, nutrition is the melody and training is the dance. Both are inseparably connected and complement each other to create a harmonious whole. In the previous chapters, we focused on how a plant-based diet nourishes and strengthens your body. Now, it's time to take this well-oiled engine onto the road – with a training plan tailored to your individual goals, abilities, and needs.

In this chapter, we open the door to a world where your vegan lifestyle and your training regime go hand in hand. We delve into the art and science of training and provide you with practical tools and insights to create a workout plan that is as unique and dynamic as your life. From constructing a workout plan to monitoring your progress, this chapter is your personal coach guiding you through the nuances of training planning.

The workout plans you create here are not just a scheme of exercises but a reflection of your life philosophy – one that respects reverence for life and mirrors your decision for a vegan diet. Whether you want to build strength, increase endurance, or improve flexibility and mobility – we show you how to achieve your goals without compromising your values.

Prepare to take the next step. Strengthen your body, sharpen your mind, and align your training with what matters to you. Let's together shape your personal path to vegan fitness and well-being.

## Creating Workout Plans

The foundation of any successful fitness program is a well-thought-out workout plan. Like an architect drawing a blueprint, you must also plan carefully to ensure that each exercise and workout brings you closer to your goal. In this section, we'll show you how to create a workout plan that is not only effective and efficient but also sustainable and enjoyable.

Assessing Your Starting Point: Before diving into training, it's crucial to take stock. Assess your current fitness level, including your strengths and areas needing improvement. This could involve a mix of cardiovascular endurance, muscle strength, flexibility, and overall physical performance.

Define Your Fitness Goals: Clear goals are key to motivation and success. Whether you're preparing for a marathon, building muscle, or just wanting to stay active – your goals should be SMART: Specific, Measurable, Achievable, Relevant, and Time-bound.

Personalizing Your Workout Plan: Your workout plan should be as unique as you are. Consider your lifestyle, schedule, and personal preferences. Some may enjoy the tranquility of a long morning run, while others prefer the energy of an evening group fitness class. Choose activities that bring you joy to ensure longevity.

Integrating Vegan Nutrition: Nutrition plays a central role in achieving your fitness goals. A well-tuned vegan diet can provide the necessary energy for your workouts and support quick recovery. Pay attention to a balanced intake of macro and micronutrients and adjust your calorie intake to your training volume.

Variety and Periodization: Avoid monotony by introducing variety in your workout plan. Implementing periodization, i.e., alternating phases of load and recovery, can help you avoid overtraining and achieve continuous progress. This may also mean combining different forms of training to achieve holistic fitness levels.

Monitoring Progress and Seeking Expert Advice: Keeping a training diary or using specialized apps can provide valuable insights into your progress and the effectiveness of your workout plan. While self-observation and initiative play an important role, seeking expert advice can also be enriching. At Gentle Vegan, we understand that every body and fitness journey is unique. Our experts in vegan fitness coaching can help refine, adjust, and ensure that your plan meets your specific nutritional and training requirements. Don't hesitate to rely on our experience and knowledge to achieve your goals in the most effective and enjoyable way.

With these steps as a foundation, you can create a workout plan that not only leads to your fitness goal but also harmonizes with your vegan lifestyle. In the next subchapter, we will delve deeper into how specific training routines can be developed for different fitness goals.

## Training Routines for Different Fitness Goals

Designing your workout plan is a creative and scientific process that should align with your individual fitness goals. It's important to ensure close coordination between your vegan dietary regime and the chosen training approach. In the following, we will illuminate the nuances of workout planning for different goals and how you can smartly combine these with a plant-based diet.

### Strength Building and Muscle Synthesis

The aim of strength training is to increase muscle strength and size. It begins with a structured workout plan that includes compound exercises like squats, bench presses, and deadlifts. These exercises activate multiple muscle groups simultaneously and are effective for muscle building. An optimal regimen could involve heavy lifting three to four times a week with periodization, varying resistance and volume over time to avoid plateaus and encourage continuous growth.

Adequate protein intake, especially post-workout, is essential for the repair and growth of muscle fibers. Here, the vegan diet can play a crucial role with targeted meals rich in complete proteins – for instance, combinations of quinoa and beans.

### Endurance Enhancement and Cardiovascular Health

Endurance training aims to improve the efficiency of the cardiovascular system. Running, cycling, or swimming training can be structured at varying intensities. Long-distance training at moderate intensity forms the base, while high-intensity interval training

(HIIT) can be incorporated to increase maximum oxygen uptake (VO2 max).

The associated nutritional strategy should include a higher carbohydrate intake to replenish glycogen stores and provide energy for longer endurance sessions. Foods with complex carbohydrates like whole grains, sweet potatoes, and lentils offer sustainable energy.

## Flexibility, Mobility, and Joint Health

Flexibility training aims to maintain and improve the range of motion of joints and reduce the risk of injuries. Yoga and Pilates are popular practices that address both physical and mental components. Incorporating flexibility training into your daily routine can work wonders not only for joint health but also for stress reduction and overall well-being.

An anti-inflammatory diet, rich in Omega-3 fatty acids from sources like walnuts and flaxseeds, supports joint health and can help optimize flexibility and mobility.

In intertwining these training components with your vegan lifestyle, it's crucial to pay attention to your body's signals and seek professional support if you're unsure. A customized workout plan, shaped by the expertise of our Gentle Vegan coaches, can ensure not only better performance but also sustain your motivation and joy in movement.

Through interactive engagement with our experts, you can ensure that your workout routine works not just on paper but in practice, and that you not only reach but exceed your goals. Gentle Vegan is by your side to perfect the synchronicity of body, mind, and nutrition – for fitness that is based on compassion and science.

## Adapting Workout Plans to Lifestyle

To sustainably integrate a workout plan into your daily life, it needs to be flexible, individual, and realistic. Here are comprehensive strategies on how you can harmonize your fitness goals with the demands of your lifestyle, while still allowing enough room for personal development and recovery.

Personal Time Analysis: Start with a thorough analysis of your typical daily and weekly routines. Identify gaps that can be consistently used for training, and consider underutilized times that could be opened up through more efficient time management.

Adaptation to Circadian Rhythms and Energy Levels: Consider your personal biorhythm. Are you a morning person or do you feel more energized in the evening? Adjust your training to coincide with your natural energy peaks to maximize effectiveness.

Micro-Workouts: If longer training sessions are difficult to realize, divide your training into several short, so-called "micro-workouts" throughout the day. These can focus on specific muscle groups or fitness components such as strength, endurance, or flexibility.

Integrating Training into Daily Life: Turn everyday activities into training opportunities. Stand up during phone calls and do squats, use your lunch break for a quick walk, or integrate bodyweight exercises while waiting for the kettle to boil.

Family and Partner Workouts: If you want to spend time with your family or partner, plan joint activities that also count as a workout. This can range from bike rides to hiking to playful sports like beach volleyball.

Prioritization and Boundary Setting: Decide what priorities to set and where to draw boundaries. It may be necessary to say "no" to things that are less important in order to ensure enough time for your health and fitness.

Preparation for Unpredictabilities: Create emergency training plans for days when unforeseen events disrupt your normal schedule. Short high-intensity interval training (HIIT) workouts or yoga sessions at home can be ideal alternatives.

Goal Alignment and Flexibility: Set clear goals and adjust training plans accordingly. If your goals change, be ready to adapt your training plan. This may mean intensifying, shortening, or varying certain training phases.

Technology as a Supporter: Use technology like apps that help you track your progress, plan and optimize workouts. Online training programs or virtual trainers can also support you when you can't go to the gym.

Professional Tips and Coaching: Consider getting professional support. Coaches from Gentle Vegan can create training plans perfectly tailored to your lifestyle and support you in implementation. They can also act as accountability partners and help you stay on track.

Integrating fitness into your lifestyle should be seen not as a burden, but as an enrichment. A well-adapted workout plan takes into account your personal circumstances and helps you improve your health and well-being without neglecting other areas of life.

# Monitoring Progress and Making Adjustments

Having an effective training plan is just the beginning of your fitness journey. Continuously monitoring and adjusting your plan is crucial to ensure that you stay on the best path to your goals. It's not just about improving performance, but also about maintaining your health and motivation. Key aspects to consider include:

Listening to Body Feedback: While numbers and statistics are valuable tools to measure progress, they don't tell the whole story. Pay attention to your body and heed warning signs like chronic fatigue, pain, or decreasing motivation. These could indicate overtraining, insufficient recovery, or suboptimal nutrition. Adjustments might involve reducing training sessions, lowering intensity, or focusing more on recovery and sleep.

Mental and Emotional Balance: Your mental health plays a central role in training success. Stress, lack of motivation, and burnout are serious factors that can impede your progress. It's important to regenerate mentally, which can be achieved through techniques like meditation, yoga, or simply through hobbies and time with friends.

Long-term Goal Setting: Make sure to contextualize short-term successes within your long-term goals. It's normal for progress to vary and not always be linear. Instead of focusing on short-term fluctuations, maintain an overview of your overall progress and make adjustments based on that.

Periodization and Variation: A training plan should never be static. Incorporate periods with different focuses, such as strength building, endurance enhancement, or technique training. This not only helps to overcome plateaus but also reduces the risk of injury by promoting different muscle groups and movement patterns.

Adaptation to Life Circumstances: If your life circumstances change, whether due to work, family, or other commitments, your training plan needs to be flexibly adapted. Ensure that your training harmonizes with your lifestyle to minimize stress and maximize enjoyment of movement.

Regular Evaluation: Set regular points for reviewing your training plan. This could be monthly or at another interval that suits you. Use these opportunities to reflect on what's going well and what could be improved. Based on this evaluation, you can decide whether to continue your training plan as planned, modify it, or even redesign it entirely.

Incorporating Expertise: Don't hesitate to consult experts if you feel stuck or have specific health concerns. Professional trainers, physiotherapists, or nutritionists can provide valuable insights and guidance to help you optimize your plan and tailor it to your personal needs.

Monitoring and adjusting your training plan is a dynamic process that requires your mindfulness and commitment. With a balanced strategy that encompasses both physical and psychological aspects, you create a solid foundation for long-term success and well-being.

GENTLE VEGAN

# Chapter 08

# Tips, Tricks, and Common Challenges

# Overview and Handling of Challenges

Transitioning to a plant-based lifestyle and integrating it into your fitness routine often comes with questions, doubts, and challenges. This chapter not only addresses common concerns but also discusses strategies that help you stay motivated, make progress, and not be discouraged by common misconceptions.

Veganism in fitness is not a new phenomenon, but it is one that is often misunderstood. The following sections provide you with well-founded insights and practical solutions, based on scientific findings and the experiences of numerous vegan athletes. You will learn how to find support in the vegan community, overcome everyday hurdles, and fully exploit the benefits of a plant-based diet. With Gentle Vegan by your side, you are prepared to design your diet and training in a way that they support each other and lead you to your best physical condition.

# Addressing Common Objections and Misconceptions

Embarking on a vegan fitness journey, you will undoubtedly encounter a range of objections and misconceptions. Concerns about nutrient deficiencies, energy loss, or inadequate protein intake are not uncommon. The key is to be well-informed and able to distinguish facts from myths. This knowledge will not only reinforce your own decision but also enable you to communicate effectively and provide support when encountering skepticism.

## Protein: The Pervasive Myth

Proteins often become a focal point in discussions about vegan diets. Fortunately, there are numerous plant-based protein sources, from lentils and beans to tofu and seitan. The trick is to diversify protein intake to ensure a full spectrum of amino acids. Additionally, many plant-based protein powders on the market can supplement your diet. We'll show you how to meet your protein needs without compromising on variety and taste.

## Iron, Calcium, and Other Nutrients

Another common misconception concerns the intake

of iron and calcium. Many fear that the absence of meat and dairy inevitably leads to deficiencies. In reality, however, many plants, including leafy greens, nuts, seeds, and whole grains, contain both iron and calcium. Consuming vitamin C-rich foods can also enhance iron absorption. We'll guide you through the best combinations and show you how a balanced, plant-based diet provides all the necessary nutrients.

## Energy and Endurance

Concerns that a vegan diet might not provide enough energy for strenuous workouts are also widespread. However, this can be easily dispelled by considering the abundance of carbohydrate-rich foods in a vegan diet. Carbohydrates are the body's primary energy source, and foods like sweet potatoes, quinoa, whole-grain pasta, and fruits are excellent fuel sources. We'll give you tips on how to time your meals optimally to keep your energy levels high.

## The Transition Process

It's important to acknowledge that transitioning to a vegan diet takes time. Your body may need a period of adjustment to get used to the new sources of energy. Just like training, nutrition is a matter of habit and conditioning. Patience and perseverance are key here. We'll help you navigate this transition with understanding and patience for your body.

### Building a Strong Foundation

Gentle Vegan understands these challenges and is ready to provide you with sound knowledge and practical tools. Through our guidance, recipes, and personal consultations, we'll show you how to lay a solid foundation for your vegan fitness journey. With the right information and a dash of creativity, you'll be able to not only refute objections and misconceptions but also transform them into opportunities for education and growth.

Armed with this knowledge, you are well-equipped to dispel common misconceptions and inspire others on their path to a healthier, plant-based lifestyle. In the next section, we'll focus on how to apply these foundations and maintain your motivation to facilitate a lasting transition to a vegan diet.

## Tips for Getting Started and Maintaining Motivation

Embarking on a vegan fitness journey can be both exhilarating and daunting. It's a time of learning and experimenting, requiring adaptability and resolve. To ease your start, we have compiled a series of tips to not only help you take your first steps but also to keep your motivation strong in the long run.

### Finding Your Personal Why

Your "why" is the core of your motivation, the deep, personal reason that led you to the vegan lifestyle. Whether it's health benefits, animal welfare, or environmental concerns – regularly remind yourself of these reasons. They are the foundation upon which you build and to which you can return when you need a reminder of your goals.

### Setting Realistic Goals

Start with clear, achievable goals tailored to your current capabilities and life circumstances. Setting SMART goals – specific, measurable, achievable, relevant, and time-bound – can provide a structured method to make progress and not feel overwhelmed.

### The Joy of Discovery

The vegan world is rich in diversity. Allow yourself the freedom to discover new foods and experiment with different recipes. Each meal can be an opportunity to try something new and exciting. This sense of discovery can be a powerful motivator.

## Building a Support Network

A community of like-minded individuals can be immense support. Whether online or in person, look for groups and forums where you can share experiences, seek advice, and celebrate your successes. Gentle Vegan offers a platform that introduces you to this network.

## Documenting Progress

Track your progress by keeping a nutrition and training journal or taking regular photos. Visible evidence of your development can remind you of how far you've come and serve as motivation to keep going.

## Developing a Sustainable Routine

Consistency is key to success. Gradually build habits that are integrable into your daily life and can be sustained in the long term. A routine helps make your vegan fitness practices second nature.

## Maintaining a Flexible Attitude

Flexibility in dealing with setbacks or unforeseen events is important. Be lenient with yourself when things don't go as planned, and be ready to adjust your strategies to stay on track.

## Utilizing Sources of Inspiration

Read stories of vegan athletes, listen to podcasts, or

watch documentaries about vegan fitness. These can serve as daily doses of inspiration and offer new perspectives and motivation.

### Gentle Vegan as Your Guide

Utilize the resources and coaching Gentle Vegan offers. From personal consultations to tailored nutrition plans, we are here to help you overcome hurdles and achieve your goals.

By embracing these tips, you create a solid foundation for your success. Remember that every journey is unique and your personal growth is just as valuable as the final goal. With patience, dedication, and the right resources, your vegan fitness journey will be sustainable, fulfilling, and joyful.

## Strategies for Overcoming Obstacles

Every journey is paved with challenges, and the path to a vegan fitness lifestyle is no exception. Whether they are personal, social, or physical hurdles, the ability to overcome obstacles is crucial for long-term success and satisfaction. Here are some strategies to help you navigate common stumbling blocks.

### Knowledge as a Tool

Educate yourself thoroughly about vegan nutrition and fitness to counter common myths and misconceptions. Knowledge builds confidence in your decisions and prepares you to respond factually to criticism or questions about your lifestyle.

### Planning and Preparation

Good planning is key to avoiding difficulties. Preparation might mean cooking meals in advance, always having a vegan snack option on hand, or blocking out your training routine in your calendar. Being prepared leaves less room for excuses and unforeseen circumstances.

### Cultivating a Positive Mindset

The attitude with which you face challenges can make a big difference. A positive mindset helps you see obstacles as opportunities for growth. Practice gratitude for your body and the progress you have made to empower yourself.

### Accepting Small Steps

Understand that not every step needs to be huge. Accept small progress and recognize that it is also part of the path to success. Every small decision for a plant-based meal or completed workout counts.

## Practicing Self-Care

Pay attention to the signals from your body and mind. If you feel overwhelmed, take a break. Self-care practices like meditation, yoga, or just a relaxing bath can help reduce stress and rejuvenate you.

## Seeking Support

Don't hesitate to ask for help, whether from friends, family, or professional coaches. A support system can be a safe haven when the waves get high. Gentle Vegan also offers coaching and consultation to find solutions together.

## Demonstrating Adaptability

Be willing to change your plan when your life changes. Flexibility allows you to respond to long-term changes in your life, such as a new job or family commitments, without giving up your vegan fitness goals.

## Celebrating Your Successes

Don't forget to celebrate your victories, no matter how small they may be. Celebrate buying a new vegan cookbook collection, achieving a new fitness goal, or simply getting through a tough day.

### Using Setbacks as Learning Opportunities

If you stumble or experience a setback, don't be too hard on yourself. Take time to reflect on what didn't work and use these insights to become stronger in the future.

By implementing these strategies, you will be better equipped to handle the inevitable challenges on your path. Remember, every setback is only temporary, and with the right attitude and appropriate tools, you can continue to progress and achieve your goals.

## How Gentle Vegan Can Support You

At Gentle Vegan, we are committed to a holistic approach in supporting your journey towards a healthier and more compassionate lifestyle. Here's an overview of how we can assist you in your pursuit of vegan fitness:

### Personal Coaching

Our cornerstone service is personal coaching, where

we cater to your individual needs. Our experts guide you step by step, whether it's transitioning to a vegan diet, integrating fitness into your daily life, or overcoming personal challenges along the way to your goals.

### Nutritional Consultation

Focusing on the right balance of macro and micronutrients in a vegan diet, we offer tailored consultation to ensure your body gets all the essential nutrients it needs for building muscle strength and endurance.

### Access to Resources

We provide you with comprehensive eBooks and articles that delve deep into the world of vegan nutrition and fitness. These resources are always accessible and offer valuable information to support your lifestyle.

### Sustainable Products and Unique Designs

Explore our carefully curated selection of sustainably crafted textiles and items made from recycled materials in our shop. Each design results from a creative collaboration with vegan artists, reflecting the connection between aesthetics and vegan ethics. Contribute to a responsible lifestyle with our limited collections and express your connection to the vegan movement stylishly.

## Online Community

Our online community is a vital part of our offering. Here, you have the opportunity to connect with other members, find inspiration and motivation, and be part of a supportive and positive group.

## Customer Service

Our dedicated team is ready to assist you with any questions about our products and services. We place a high value on customer satisfaction and strive to make your experience with Gentle Vegan as enriching and hassle-free as possible.

At Gentle Vegan, our goal is to offer you not just products and services but also a source of inspiration and information. We are here to support and empower you so that you can achieve your fitness and life goals in a sustainable and ethical way.

GENTLE VEGAN

## Chapter 09

# Stories of Vegan Athletes

# Jacqueline Otchere

Jacqueline Otchere, an outstanding German pole vaulter, embodies a rare combination of athletic excellence and deeply rooted personal convictions. Born on May 5, 1996, in Heidelberg, she has made her mark not only in her sporting discipline but also through her vegan lifestyle and commitment to environmental and animal protection.

Her athletic journey began at the age of eight in track and field, where she initially shone in sprinting and jumping disciplines. Her later specialization in pole vaulting proved to be a wise decision that led her to new heights. With impressive personal bests of 4.30 meters indoors and 4.60 meters outdoors, multiple gold medals at German Championships, and significant international appearances, she has established herself as one of the leading athletes in this discipline.

Besides her athletic career, Otchere pursued a degree in biosciences at Heidelberg University, which she successfully completed in 2023. Her decision to adopt a vegan diet, influenced by a documentary on factory farming, initially posed a challenge, especially considering her coach's skepticism. However, Otchere demonstrated that a plant-based diet is not only viable but also beneficial in competitive sports. Thus, she serves as a role model for many considering a vegan lifestyle, especially in the context of high-performance sports.

Her love for animals and commitment to environmental protection extend beyond sports. As part of the 'Sports for Future' initiative, she advocates for climate protection and sustainability. Her efforts to reduce plastic waste and lead a conscious life reflect her commitment to these critical issues.

Jacqueline Otchere thus exemplifies the integration of athletic excellence with personal beliefs and social engagement. Her achievements in pole vaulting and her advocacy for a sustainable, ethical way of living make her a remarkable personality, offering inspiration and a role model far beyond the realms of sports.

## Patrik Baboumian

Patrik Baboumian, an exceptional strength athlete and non-fiction author of Armenian descent, represents a remarkable blend of athletic prowess and deeply rooted ethical convictions. Born on July 1, 1979, in Abadan, Iran, he has not only established himself as one of Germany's strongest men but also gained recognition for his vegan lifestyle and commitment to animal rights and environmental protection.

Baboumian's athletic career began at the age of 15 when he turned to strength sports. His journey led him from bodybuilding to Strongman competitions, where he broke numerous records and won the title 'Germany's Strongest Man' in 2011. His impressive achievements in strength sports, including world records in log lifting and the Yoke Walk, attest to his extraordinary physical strength and discipline.

In addition to his sporting career, Baboumian studied psychology and successfully graduated, highlighting his intellectual curiosity and versatility. His decision to adopt a vegan diet in 2011 was initially a challenge in strength sports. However, he proved that a plant-based diet is not only viable but also conducive to peak performance in sports. Baboumian thus serves as a role model for many considering a vegan lifestyle, especially in the context of high-performance sports.

His commitment to animal rights and environmental protection extends far beyond sports. Baboumian, who appeared in the documentary 'The Game Changers,' actively opposes speciesism and promotes awareness of the importance of a sustainable and ethical lifestyle. His efforts to change public perception regarding veganism in sports reflect his dedication to these important issues.

Patrik Baboumian exemplifies the integration of athletic excellence with personal beliefs and social engagement. His achievements in strength sports and his advocacy for a sustainable, ethical way of living make him a remarkable personality, offering inspiration and a role model far beyond the realms of sports.

## Mac Danzig

Mac Danzig, a former professional mixed martial artist and committed vegan, represents a remarkable synthesis of athletic excellence and deep ethical convictions. Born on January 2, 1980, in Cleveland, Ohio, Danzig has made a name for himself not only in the world of combat sports but also as an influential advocate for a vegan lifestyle and an activist for animal rights.

His journey into the world of mixed martial arts was marked by an early passion for martial arts. This passion, combined with talent and dedication, led him to a successful career in various MMA organizations, including the prestigious Ultimate Fighting Championship (UFC). In the UFC, he distinguished himself through technical finesse and strategic combat leadership, earning respect and recognition in the MMA community

Danzig's decision to adopt a vegan lifestyle for ethical reasons and out of respect for animals and the environment posed challenges in a sport traditionally dominated by a protein-rich, meat-based diet. Despite initial skepticism, he proved that it is possible to compete at the highest level while maintaining a plant-based diet. His diet includes a variety of foods such as brown rice, mushrooms, tempeh, quinoa, beans, and lentils, and he places great emphasis on balanced protein intake.

Outside the ring, Danzig uses his platform to advocate for the benefits of a vegan lifestyle and to raise greater awareness for animal rights. His commitment to veganism and animal rights extends far beyond sports, making him a role model for many who aspire to a sustainable and responsible way of living.

Mac Danzig, therefore, exemplifies the integration of athletic excellence and deeply rooted ethical convictions. His successes in MMA and his tireless efforts for veganism and animal rights make him an inspiring figure who garners recognition and admiration both in the world of sports and the vegan community.

# Alex Morgan

Alex Morgan, an outstanding soccer player and dedicated vegan, is a shining example of the connection between athletic excellence and strong ethical convictions. Born on July 2, 1989, in Diamond Bar, California, Morgan has not only established herself as one of the most successful players of her generation in women's soccer but also as an advocate for a plant-based diet and an activist for animal rights.

Morgan's soccer career began at the University of California, Berkeley, where she played for the California Golden Bears. Her exceptional talent led her to be the number one pick in 2011 for the Western New York Flash and later to other prestigious teams such as Orlando Pride and Olympique Lyon. Her impressive performances, including victories at the FIFA Women's World Cups in 2015 and 2019 and a silver medal at the 2012 London Olympics, attest to her outstanding athletic ability.

In addition to her sporting achievements, Morgan is also known for her vegan convictions. She opted for a vegan diet in 2017, motivated by her love for animals and the desire to lead a more ethical lifestyle. This decision also had positive effects on her athletic performance and well-being. Morgan reports improved mental clarity, increased physical fitness, and faster recovery after training.

Morgan is not only active on the field but also uses her platform to raise awareness of the benefits of a vegan lifestyle and to advocate for animal rights. She is a role model for many who aspire to a sustainable and responsible way of living and demonstrates that peak performance in sports is possible with a plant-based diet.

Alex Morgan thus stands as a symbol of the integration of athletic excellence and deeply rooted ethical convictions. Her successes on the soccer field and her commitment to veganism and animal rights make her an inspiring personality who garners recognition both in the world of sports and the vegan community.

GENTLE VEGAN

# Chapter 10

# FAQs Frequently Asked Questions

# General Questions About the Vegan Lifestyle and Fitness

In this section, we answer frequently asked questions (FAQs) that help you better understand the vegan lifestyle, especially in connection with fitness and sports. These questions have been carefully selected to clarify typical uncertainties and misunderstandings that often occur when switching to a vegan diet.

## What are the basic principles of a vegan lifestyle?

A vegan lifestyle goes beyond mere diet. It is a comprehensive philosophy that aims to avoid consuming products of animal origin, whether in diet, clothing, or other areas of life. This is based on the desire to cause no harm to animals and to promote a more environmentally friendly and sustainable way of living.

## How can I ensure that I receive all the necessary nutrients as a vegan?

A balanced vegan diet can provide all necessary nutrients. It is important to consume a variety of foods, including vegetables, fruits, legumes, nuts, seeds, and whole grains. Supplements like vitamin B12, vitamin D, and omega-3 fatty acids may be considered to ensure complete nutrient coverage.

### Can I get enough protein for muscle building as a vegan?

Yes, there are many plant-based protein sources such as legumes, tofu, seitan, tempeh, nuts, and seeds. These foods can be consumed in sufficient quantities to meet the protein needs of an active lifestyle, including muscle building.

### Is a vegan diet suitable for all types of fitness goals?

A vegan diet can be suitable for a variety of fitness goals, from weight loss to muscle building to improved overall health and endurance. The key is to adjust the diet to your specific goals and needs.

### How do I start with a vegan lifestyle?

Transitioning to a vegan lifestyle is an individual process. A good start can be to gradually replace animal products with plant-based alternatives and try out new vegan recipes. Educate yourself about vegan nutrition, and consider professional advice to ensure that your diet remains balanced.

### How do I deal with social situations where non-vegan options dominate?

In social situations, it can be helpful to plan ahead, for example, by suggesting restaurants with vegan options or bringing your own vegan dishes to events. Open communication with friends and family about your dietary choices can also be beneficial.

These FAQs serve as a solid foundation for anyone looking to understand and embrace the vegan lifestyle in connection with fitness and sports. With these answers, you are well-equipped to make informed decisions and successfully integrate a vegan lifestyle.

## Specific Nutritional Questions

In this section, we delve into more specific aspects of vegan nutrition relevant to fitness enthusiasts. These answers aim to create a deeper understanding of how to optimally tailor your diet to your training goals.

### How do I plan vegan meals for optimal performance?

For optimal performance, it's important to plan meals around training sessions. Before training, focus on carbohydrate-rich foods to provide energy, while post-training, a combination of proteins and carbohydrates is ideal for supporting recovery and muscle building.

### Which vegan foods are particularly good for recovery?

Foods rich in antioxidants, proteins, and healthy fats are particularly beneficial for supporting recovery. Berries, dark leafy greens, nuts and seeds, and legumes are excellent options to reduce inflammation and promote muscle repair.

### Are there vegan foods that are particularly energy-dense?

Yes, certain vegan foods are particularly nutrient- and energy-dense. These include avocados, quinoa, oats, nuts, and dried fruits. They can be excellent options to maintain your energy during intense training sessions.

### How can I maintain my electrolyte balance as a vegan?

Electrolytes are essential for many body functions, especially during intense training. Coconut water, bananas, sweet potatoes, and various salts (like Himalayan salt) are good natural sources to supplement electrolytes like potassium, sodium, and magnesium.

### How do I deal with cravings, especially for non-vegan foods?

Cravings can be a sign that your body is missing certain nutrients. Ensure you are consuming enough calories and a wide range of nutrients. For specific cravings, there are often vegan alternatives that can help satisfy them without deviating from your vegan diet.

### Are there specific dietary recommendations for vegan endurance athletes?

Vegan endurance athletes should ensure they consume enough complex carbohydrates for sustained energy and sufficient proteins for recovery. Hydration and maintaining electrolyte balance are also crucial.

By considering these specific nutritional aspects, you can ensure that your vegan diet optimally supports your physical performance and well-being.

## Questions on Training and Exercises

In this section, we address specific questions related to training and exercises within the context of a vegan lifestyle. This information aims to help you effectively shape your training program and harmonize it with your vegan diet.

## How does the training program for vegans differ from non-vegans?

Fundamentally, there are no major differences in training programs between vegans and non-vegans. The key is to tailor the training to individual goals and needs, regardless of dietary habits. However, vegans should pay special attention to ensuring their diet supports their energy needs and recovery.

## What type of training is best suited for vegan fitness enthusiasts?

Vegan fitness enthusiasts can benefit from a variety of training types, whether it's strength training, endurance training, HIIT (High-Intensity Interval Training), or flexibility and balance exercises. The choice of training depends on individual goals, preferences, and fitness levels.

## Are there specific recovery techniques that vegans should use after training?

Post-training, it's important to nourish the body with the right nutrients, especially proteins and carbohydrates, to support recovery. Stretching exercises, drinking plenty of water, and possibly yoga or meditation can also contribute to regeneration.

### Can I build the same muscle mass and strength as a non-vegan as a vegan?

Yes, vegans can build comparable muscle mass and strength. Adequate intake of calories and protein, along with tailored strength training, is crucial. Plant-based proteins can be as effective as animal proteins when it comes to muscle building.

### How can I ensure that I have enough energy for my training as a vegan?

Ensure that your diet includes sufficient complex carbohydrates, as these are the primary energy source for your training. Whole grains, legumes, fruits, and vegetables are excellent sources of energy.

### Are there specific training tips for vegans interested in weight loss?

For vegans looking to lose weight, it's important to create a caloric deficit while still ensuring all nutritional needs are met. A combination of cardiovascular training and strength training can be effective in burning fat while maintaining muscle mass.

By understanding these specific aspects, you can ensure that your training program and vegan diet work hand in hand to achieve your fitness goals.

# Mental and Emotional Support

In this section, we focus on questions about mental and emotional support, particularly relevant to those pursuing a vegan lifestyle in the context of fitness and sports. This information aims to help overcome the psychological challenges that can accompany this way of life.

## How do I handle criticism or misunderstanding from family and friends about my vegan lifestyle?

It's important to deal with criticism or misunderstanding patiently and empathetically. Listen to their concerns and share your reasons for choosing a vegan lifestyle in an informative and non-confrontational manner. Networking with a supportive community to share experiences and find backing can also be helpful.

## How can I stay motivated when results are not immediately visible?

Mental strength is crucial when pursuing long-term goals. Set realistic, achievable goals and celebrate small progresses. Remember your reasons for choosing the vegan lifestyle and that changes take time.

## How can I cope with the feeling of being "left out" that can arise from a vegan lifestyle?

Feeling excluded as a vegan is not uncommon. Try to find activities and social circles where your lifestyle is supported and accepted. Online communities and local vegan groups can also offer a sense of belonging and support.

## How can I manage stress and overwhelm due to nutritional planning and fitness management?

Plan ahead and set realistic expectations. It's important to find a balance between dietary discipline and enjoying life. Allow yourself flexibility and be gentle with yourself. Stress management techniques like meditation, yoga, or simple breathing exercises can also be helpful.

## Are there strategies to promote a positive self-image, especially in a performance-driven fitness culture?

Building a positive self-image requires conscious efforts. Focus on your own progress and strengths instead of comparing yourself to others. Positive self-talk and mindfulness exercises can help in fostering self-acceptance and love.

## How can I maintain my emotional well-being while pursuing a vegan fitness lifestyle?

Your emotional well-being is as important as your physical health. Take time out for activities that delight and relax you. Ensure adequate sleep, social interactions, and time in nature to promote holistic well-being.

These tips are intended to help you maintain a balanced perspective and stay both mentally and emotionally strong while pursuing your vegan fitness lifestyle.

GENTLE VEGAN

# Chapter 11

# Resources And Further Information

# Book Recommendations and Professional Literature

In this section, we would like to highlight some valuable resources that provide deeper insights into vegan living and fitness. These books and professional literature are carefully selected to offer you comprehensive information and inspiration.

## "The Plant-Based Athlete" by Robert Cheeke and Matt Frazier

This book offers a comprehensive guide for athletes interested in a plant-based diet. It includes not just nutritional guidelines but also training plans and success stories from professional athletes who live vegan.

## "Vegan for Life" by Jack Norris and Virginia Messina

As a comprehensive guide to vegan nutrition, this book covers all important aspects, from ensuring adequate nutrient intake to practical everyday tips. It is especially helpful for those who want to learn comprehensively about the health aspects of veganism.

### "Thrive: The Vegan Nutrition Guide" by Brendan Brazier

Written by a former professional triathlete, this book focuses on performance enhancement through vegan nutrition. Brazier presents a holistic approach that includes stress management and sleep.

### "How Not to Die" by Dr. Michael Greger

In his book, Dr. Greger provides a scientifically based insight into the health benefits of a plant-based diet. He explores how certain foods and dietary habits can prevent and even reverse diseases.

### "Vegan Fitness for Mortals" by Ellen Jaffe Jones

This book is aimed at everyday fitness enthusiasts and offers practical advice on integrating vegan nutrition into a regular training program. It is ideal for readers looking for realistic and actionable tips.

### "The Ultimate Guide to a Plant-Powered Life" by Michael Markens

For more in-depth reading, we also recommend "The Ultimate Guide to a Plant-Powered Life" by Michael Markens. This book is an excellent resource for anyone looking to delve deeper into the world of veganism. Markens combines scientific research with practical advice, providing a comprehensive overview of the health, ecological, and ethical benefits of a plant-based lifestyle. Whether you are just starting out or are more advanced, this book offers valuable insights and guidance to enrich and strengthen your vegan lifestyle.

By reading these books, you can expand your knowledge, find inspiration, and develop practical strategies to optimally combine your vegan lifestyle with your fitness goals.

# Online-Ressources and Communities

In this section, we present a selection of online resources and communities that can support you on your vegan fitness journey. These platforms offer a wealth of information, inspiration, and the opportunity to connect with like-minded individuals.

## Vegan Fitness and Nutrition Forums

Vegan Bodybuilding & Fitness: A comprehensive platform specifically for vegan bodybuilders and fitness enthusiasts. Here you can find discussion forums, success stories, and advice from experienced vegan athletes.

Plant-Based Fitness Forum: An online forum focused on plant-based nutrition and fitness. Members can share training plans, nutrition tips, and recipes.

## Social Media Groups

Facebook and LinkedIn Groups: There are numerous groups on social platforms dedicated to vegan nutrition and fitness. These groups are great places to get tips, ask questions, and be inspired by others.

Instagram and YouTube Channels: Many vegans and fitness enthusiasts share their journeys, recipes, and workouts on Instagram and YouTube. These can be a source of inspiration and learning.

## Blogs and Websites

No Meat Athlete: A website with a blog, podcast, and resources for plant-based runners and athletes. The content ranges from training plans to nutrition tips.

Oh She Glows: A popular blog offering a variety of vegan recipes that are both nutritious and delicious. Ideal for those looking to expand their vegan cooking.

## Online Courses and Webinars

Many nutrition experts and fitness coaches offer online courses and webinars focusing on vegan nutrition and fitness. These can be particularly helpful for gaining in-depth knowledge and practical guidance.

### Vegan Fitness Apps

There are various apps specifically designed to support vegan dietary plans and workouts. These apps can be very useful in planning meals, tracking macronutrients, and structuring workouts.

Utilizing these online resources and immersing yourself in communities can be a great support on your journey to a healthy and active vegan lifestyle. They offer not only valuable information and guidance but also the opportunity to share experiences and find support.

## Apps and Tools for Vegan Fitness

In this section, we recommend various apps and digital tools that can help you optimize your vegan fitness journey. These resources provide support in areas such as nutritional planning, workout tracking, and knowledge building.

### Nutritional Tracking Apps

Cronometer: This app allows you to log your daily food intake and ensure you're getting all the necessary nutrients. It's particularly useful for keeping an eye on macro and micronutrients.

MyFitnessPal: With an extensive food database, MyFitnessPal makes it easy to track calories and macronutrients. You can add your own meals and tailor the app to your specific vegan needs.

### Fitness Tracking Apps

Strava: Ideal for runners, cyclists, and swimmers to track workouts, analyze progress, and connect with a community of sports enthusiasts.

Fitbit: Although not specifically vegan, Fitbit offers comprehensive tracking features for activities, sleep patterns, and even nutrition, making it a valuable tool for fitness management.

### Recipe and Meal Planning Apps

Forks Over Knives: This app offers a variety of vegan recipes and helpful meal planning tips based on the namesake documentary and book.

HappyCow: An indispensable resource for finding vegan restaurants and stores worldwide, especially useful when traveling.

### Educational and Information Apps

Daily Dozen by Dr. Michael Greger: An app based on Dr. Greger's recommendations, helping you ensure you consume a variety of healthy vegan foods daily.

Audible: Audiobooks and podcasts about vegan nutrition and fitness can be a great source of information and inspiration. Audible offers a wide range of relevant titles.

These apps and tools can help you achieve your goals by providing useful information and tracking features. By utilizing these digital resources, you can make your vegan lifestyle and fitness goals more effective and efficient.

# Contact Gentle Vegan and Coaching Offers

Gentle Vegan represents a lifestyle that harmonizes health, ethics, and sustainability, aiming to enhance both individual well-being and global awareness. Our philosophy is based on the belief that through knowledge, empowerment, positivity, community, empathic strength, and sustainable action, each individual can positively impact the world. We are a platform that welcomes and supports everyone, regardless of their background, to collectively shape a conscious lifestyle.

## Personal Coaching and Consulting

We offer personal coaching aimed at supporting you on your journey to a conscious, vegan lifestyle. Our coaches provide individualized consultation and specialize in vegan nutrition, fitness, and sustainable living.

## Online Resources and Educational Material

On our website, you'll find a variety of resources, including eBooks, articles, and blogs, offering well-founded knowledge and practical tips for a vegan lifestyle. Our goal is to empower and inform you through education.

## Community and Social Networking

As part of Gentle Vegan, you benefit from an inspiring community that offers support and exchange. In our community, we foster positive changes and motivate each other to achieve our goals.

## Sustainable Products

Our range of sustainable textiles and accessories underscores our commitment to environmental protection. Each product is carefully selected to meet our high standards of quality and ethics.

## Contact and Support

For more information or personal advice, you can reach us via our website, email, or through our social media channels. Our dedicated team is always ready to answer your questions and support you on your path to a healthy, active, and ethically conscious lifestyle.

## Our homepage: gentlevegan.world

At Gentle Vegan, we combine knowledge, empathy, and sustainability to create a world where everyone can make a difference through conscious decisions and actions. We look forward to accompanying and supporting you on your journey.

GENTLE VEGAN

## Chapter 12

# Conclusion and Next Steps

# Summary of Key Points

The "Gentle Guide to Plant-Powered Fitness" provides comprehensive insights and guidance for successfully combining vegan nutrition and fitness. Here are the key points we have covered in the book:

Optimal Protein Intake: For muscle building and maintenance, it's important to consume sufficient plant-based protein sources such as legumes, nuts, seeds, and whole grains. Plant-based protein powders can also be a useful supplement.

Importance of Carbohydrates: Carbohydrates are a crucial source of energy, especially for endurance training. Whole grains, fruits, and starchy vegetables provide lasting energy and support training performance.

Healthy Fats for Energy and Recovery: Unsaturated fats from avocados, nuts, and seeds are important for overall health and aid recovery after training.

Vitamin and Mineral Intake: Adequate intake of vitamins and minerals, particularly B12, iron, calcium, and omega-3 fatty acids, is crucial for vegans. These can be ensured through a varied diet and, if necessary, supplements.

Hydration: Adequate hydration is critical for performance and recovery. Water should be the main source of hydration, supplemented with electrolyte-containing drinks during intense training.

Diversity in Training: Vegans can be successful in all types of fitness disciplines, including strength, endurance, and flexibility training. A combination of various forms of exercise promotes overall fitness and health.

Regeneration and Recovery: Adequate sleep, a balanced diet, and active recovery strategies like stretching and yoga are essential to support regeneration and prevent injuries.

Individual Adaptation: Both nutritional and training plans should be tailored to individual needs, goals, and life circumstances to ensure long-term success and satisfaction.

These points provide a foundation for designing an effective and sustainable vegan fitness lifestyle that enhances both physical performance and overall well-being.

# Inspiration and Motivation for Your Journey

The journey to a healthy, vegan lifestyle that integrates fitness and well-being can be challenging but immensely rewarding. In the "Gentle Guide to Plant-Powered Fitness," we've highlighted many aspects to inspire and motivate you on this journey. Here, we delve deeper into some of these key aspects:

Success Stories for Daily Inspiration: We've shared various inspiring stories in the book from individuals showing how diverse and enriching the path of a vegan fitness lifestyle can be. These personal narratives are intended to show you that your goals are achievable and that every step on this path counts.

The Power of Community: One of the most powerful sources of motivation is the feeling of belonging to a community. Whether online or in your local environment, exchanging ideas with like-minded individuals can open up new perspectives, provide joint solutions for challenges, and create a sense of connection.

Goal Setting and Celebrating Milestones: The

importance of clear, realistic goals cannot be overstated. By setting smaller, achievable goals and celebrating every success, you create a positive feedback loop that strengthens your motivation and encourages you to keep moving forward.

The Importance of a Long-Term Perspective: Remember that sustainable changes take time. Instead of focusing on quick fixes, concentrate on developing a lifestyle that is sustainable, healthy, and fulfilling in the long term.

Self-Care and Mindfulness Practice: It's important to take care of yourself and pay attention to your mental and emotional needs. Simple mindfulness exercises, meditation, or just conscious breaks in your daily routine can help reduce stress and bolster your overall motivation.

Continuous Learning and Adaptability: The world of veganism and fitness is dynamic and constantly evolving. Stay open to new knowledge, be willing to change your approach as your needs or circumstances change, and view each change as an opportunity for growth.

Visualization of Success: Imagine what your life will look like once you have achieved your goals. This visualization can be a powerful tool to guide and motivate you on your journey.

By integrating these motivational elements into your daily life, you can fully embrace the challenges and highlights of your vegan fitness journey. Every day offers a new opportunity to prioritize your health, well-being, and commitment to an ethical lifestyle.

## Staying Committed and Making Progress

We have provided you with the tools and knowledge to successfully pursue a vegan fitness lifestyle. But how can you ensure that you stay on this path and continuously make progress? Here are some key strategies:

Regular Review and Adjustment of Your Goals: Continuously reflecting and adjusting your goals is crucial to keep them realistic and achievable. Consider both short-term and long-term goals and adjust them according to your life circumstances. This might mean taking on new challenges or redefining goals as your priorities change.

Development and Refinement of Your Routine: A solid routine is key to maintaining your vegan fitness lifestyle. It's not just about establishing habits but also continuously refining and optimizing them. Experiment with different dietary and training plans to find what works best for your body and schedule.

Comprehensive Progress Tracking: Besides just tracking your diet and exercise, also consider other aspects like sleep quality, energy levels, and mental well-being. This holistic approach helps you develop a better understanding of how your lifestyle impacts your overall performance and health.

Constant Inspiration and Education: The world of veganism and fitness is constantly evolving. Stay informed by continuously educating yourself and getting inspired by others. This could be through attending workshops, participating in webinars, or engaging in professional forums and social media.

Strategies for Dealing with Setbacks: Recognize that setbacks are not the end of your efforts. Develop strategies to deal with disappointments, such as keeping a gratitude journal, practicing mindfulness, or talking to a mentor or coach.

Building a Support Network: A strong network of like-minded individuals, friends, family, and possibly professionals can make a tremendous difference. Consider joining a local or online community to share experiences and receive mutual support.

Celebrating and Sharing Your Successes: Sharing and celebrating your successes, both in your personal community and on social media, can be hugely motivating. This not only helps boost your self-esteem but can also inspire others.

Self-Reflection and Mindfulness: Regularly take time for self-reflection to understand your inner motivation and personal values. Mindfulness practices can help you stay aligned with your goals and beliefs.

These expanded strategies offer you a robust framework to stay motivated, overcome challenges, and achieve and maintain your goals in the vegan fitness lifestyle.

## Final Words and Encouragement

As we reach the end of "The Gentle Guide to Plant-Powered Fitness," we want to offer you some final words and encouragement. The journey you have embarked upon is more than just a change in your diet or fitness routine; it is a step towards a more conscious and fulfilling lifestyle.

Celebrate Your Courage: First, we want to congratulate you. Deciding to adopt a vegan lifestyle, especially in combination with a dedicated fitness regime, requires courage and commitment. You have taken a crucial step towards a healthier, more ethical, and sustainable way of living.

You Are Part of a Larger Movement: Remember that you are part of a growing community. Together, we contribute to a larger movement advocating for animal rights, environmental protection, and a healthier society. Every small change you make has a positive impact on the world.

The Journey Continues: This book may be ending, but your journey is not. There will be days when everything seems effortless and others when challenges may seem overwhelming. In both cases, it's important to remember why you started this path and what goals you are pursuing.

Stay Curious and Open to Growth: The world of veganism and fitness is dynamic and always evolving. Stay curious, open to new knowledge, and ready to grow. Every new insight is an opportunity to improve yourself and your practices.

You Are Not Alone: At Gentle Vegan, we are here to support you on your journey. Use our resources, join our community, and do not hesitate to seek support when you need it. We are proud to accompany you on this journey.

With these final words, we encourage you to move forward with confidence and determination. Your journey towards a vegan fitness lifestyle is an ongoing journey of discovery, learning, and growth. We wish you all the best on this path and look forward to being part of your journey.